somabasics
furniture

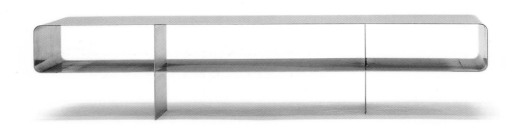

somabasics
furniture

Sebastian Conran & Mark Bond

special photography by Thomas Stewart

SOMA

To our parents, who have and will always be an inspiration

contents

Compare furniture to a poem.

Poems are constructed from words just as furniture is constructed

from details. A wrong word will jar, producing a clumsy meter,

while a poor detail will produce visual imbalance. In the same

way, in our homes a wrong piece or one in the wrong place can upset

the equilibrium of an otherwise harmonious environment.

Y's Chair, designed by Christophe Pillet in 1995 for Cappellini. This self-skinned soft polyurethane foam seat shell set on a swiveling aluminum base is a good example of harnessing technology originally developed for other purposes. Here a process used in the manufacture of car dashboards yields a comfortable yet hard-wearing seat unit.

introduction

Where did you get that chair?

Furniture has much more to it than the primary functions of support and storage. The chair we sit on and the desk we work at have undergone a great deal of thought and consideration in the way they are made, how they work and what they look like—in short, how they are designed. It is this

A stool made from reclaimed oak and designed by Christian Liaigre proves that a simply produced, basic piece of furniture can be viewed almost as a piece of sculpture.

importance of the aesthetic design that arguably makes furniture the closest that industrial design comes to fine art, often blurring the boundaries with sculpture.

From the simple austerity of the stone-age caveman to the splendor of "Grand Manner" Louis XIV décor, mankind has been making furniture and art for function and decoration for centuries. Even in today's world— a technological global village—a remote African tribesman may well fashion a simple wooden stool that would not look out of place in the stone-age caveman's humble home. In a different environmental context, perhaps set on a pedestal in a museum of contemporary art, we might view the same stool more as an objet d'art, as a celebration of elegance in simplicity adhering to the dictum "form follows function," rather than the unsophisticated and crude effort that Louis XIV's courtiers would have undoubtedly perceived it to be.

Although usually displayed and photographed in isolation, furniture is in fact rarely seen in the flattering open space of the art gallery. Furniture is intended to be used as a component of a living space in relation to other pieces. It has to function and work visually with other items around it, relating almost in the way clothes do when one dresses either for everyday or for a particular occasion. Furniture could almost be seen as clothing for our homes, with each room having a function to fulfill. If this is so, it follows that if furniture is the clothing, then lighting and art are the accessories and jewelry.

As with clothing, the agenda for furnishing our homes is as much about our own self-expression as keeping warm and feeling comfortable. Fashions continually change and there are many

*The **Wink** chair, designed by Toshiyuki Kita for Cassina, 1976–80, has a steel frame and textile-covered polyurethane foam. The soft, rounded forms of this car-seat technology–derived chaise longue are reminiscent of the works of Henry Moore.*

Egg Chair, designed by Arne Jacobsen for Fritz Hansen in 1957–58, is a fabric-covered, foam-upholstered fiberglass seat shell on a swiveling cast aluminum base with a loose seat cushion. Even the chair's name plays on its womblike antecedents. This chair has been futuristic for over forty years—only the base has shown signs of aesthetic age.

magazines dedicated to keeping you informed of the latest furnishing vogues and which designer is doing what. The fashion designer/stylist Ralph Lauren, for example, now influences the style of home furnishings as much as clothing. It seems that no fashion label, from Gucci to Banana Republic, now feels fully dressed without launching its own home-style collection.

There are "classics," too, that seem to be as perennial as Chanel's "little black dress" or Levi jeans. For instance, Charles and Ray Eames's lounge chair and ottoman (shown on page 36) and Michael Thonet's bentwood chairs (shown on page 20) are forever being rediscovered by new generations of furniture buyers. The commonality with "classics" seems to be that they all seem to spend more time in fashion than out. The reality is that clothing and home fashions are now becoming more and more inextricably linked under the broad umbrella of fashion called "lifestyle."

There is, however, one major difference between clothing and furniture. Ask yourself how much you would expect to spend on an evening out, how much on a pair of sneakers, how much on a chair. How long will the benefit of these each last?

A good night out or a pair of the latest running shoes may cost about the same as, say, a Philippe Starck dining chair. In five years, although no longer new, you may be still happy with the chair; in five months the shoes may be discarded at the back of a closet; in five days that night out is already becoming a distant memory. The fact is that the furniture fashions move at a slower pace and the benefits of a well-designed piece of furniture can be a pleasure and a treasure for a lifetime.

This book is not attempting to provide you with a comprehensive guide to the subject of furniture—merely a personal introduction. We have, however, tried to cover some of the basic issues and show what we believe to be some of the best new designs now available.

Incisa was designed by Vico Magistretti and Francesco Binfaré in 1992 for DePadova. It is a swivel armchair with rigid polyurethane structure covered in leather, upholstered with polyester wadding and with zippered, removable inner covering, set on a four-spoke base. This immaculate saddle seat has been reinterpreted with an almost Dadaist expression worthy of Marcel Duchamp himself.

getting started

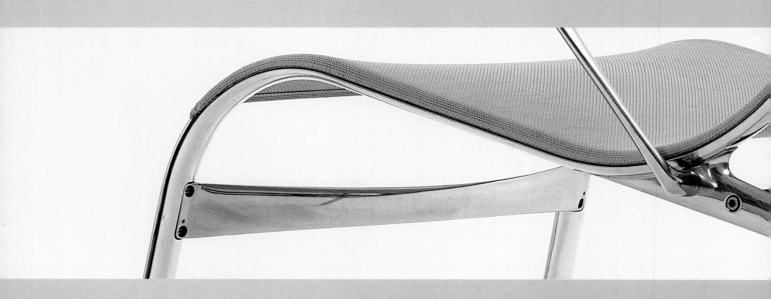

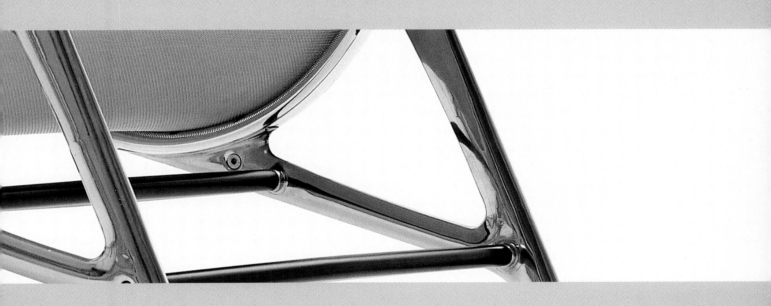

Spanish designer Javier Mariscal here demonstrates his graphic perspective with the application of asymmetrical, flat areas of color that break up the organic form in a way reminiscent of early naval camouflage. Alessandra, designed in 1995 and manufactured by Moroso, is a steel-framed chair covered with injected flame-retardant polyurethane foam, finished with natural beech legs.

getting started

Our choice of furniture and the way we use and arrange it is what makes a house into our home.

Yet home decoration is about more than satiating our inner nest-building needs; it's also another subliminal means of our self-expression—establishing our identity and reminding ourselves as well as communicating to others who we are, what we like and even which social set we subscribe to. Our homes become an inevitable extension of our identity.

Technology has also had a fundamental and permanent impact on the way we live and organize our homes. Houses were traditionally built around a very different social structure that did not encompass central heating, television or prepared meals ready for the microwave. What domestic central heating has bought us is an environment that does not require us to build fires for heat. The results of this are homes that are both

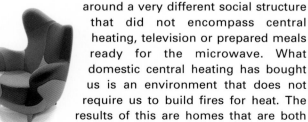

cleaner and warmer; we can have fitted carpets and flexible open spaces without drafts, thereby allowing more space for larger pieces of furniture.

The way we work and the way we live are also changing, the side effect of this being a change in the way we use our homes. The social landscape is in flux, and so, too, our relationship with our home environment. Contemporary furniture designers are fully aware of this tolerance of individuality and it is reflected in the spectrum of diversity of their approaches. Never before has there been so much collective freedom to choose from so many accessible environmental styles to put together the home that feels right for us and our aspirations.

The choice of furniture and the way it is arranged can have a dramatic effect on an otherwise indifferent space. When first considering the space to be furnished, you need to decide upon the style that suits both your personality and that of the room. The most important practical considerations are the functional use, cost, quality and aesthetic impact on the rest of the environment, closely followed by whether it will be exposed to hordes of sticky-fingered children!

This all sounds deceptively simple, but rarely do people have the option of starting completely from scratch. More often, there is a nucleus of "inherited

items" that will need careful (and sometimes brutal) editing. Decide which pieces you really love and what you will do with the things you don't (consign to the attic, auction, garage sale, dump?). Consider your lifestyle and aspirations, and what you want the room to say. Do you want it formal or comfortable? Will you want to entertain much? How many people will use the room, and for what purpose?

Consider your lifestyle and aspirations, and what you want the room to say.

Give yourself some basic rules to follow. All furniture must have a use, whether it is functional or decorative—never buy something that you cannot place, however good a bargain it may at first seem. Don't try to buy everything at once—buy one piece, place it in the room and then consider what you need to complement it. Above all, avoid clutter—a few good pieces always work better—and start with a vision.

Decide on a look that will suit the room and the building. There are many different home styles to choose from: informal, austere, original, grand, romantic. The great thing is that a different style can be used in different rooms within the same house. Don't be afraid to contrast fine, traditional details with spare, modern pieces. Think of your home as a stage.

Wood finishes and upholstered furniture will have a softer, more relaxing effect on the ambience of a room than harder, less natural materials such as glass, plastic and chrome. The choice of color and pattern as well as the type of upholstery fabric used will also have a strong influence on the practicality, appearance and identity of the furniture on which it's used, allowing strong visual coordination with the rest of the environment.

Decoration is without doubt a very important part of the function required of furniture. Consider the underlying messages conveyed, not only to others but also to yourself, as well as the superficial issues such as adherence to fashion and appearance. Too much contemporary furniture of the same style can look a little predictable and unimaginative. This can be dealt with by introducing older, interesting pieces and art to add a touch of history to the room.

Another major influence on the way a space and the furniture in it appear is the lighting. Too even an ambient light can look bland and dull. It is generally best to keep lights high or low—never in-between—so that the light is close to and reflects off the walls and ceiling. It is also good practice to create pools of light in the room by carefully placing spotlights and down-lights so that they subtly bathe the furniture pieces in light without creating glare, but with sufficient light to work or read by.

Above all, avoid clutter— a few good pieces always work better.

Placing cylindrical up-lighters on the floor or wall behind bulky pieces of furniture can produce a dramatic effect as well as increase the apparent size of the space. Also, bear in mind that the color and texture of the walls and ceiling have a strong effect on the light reflected off them.

The Polyprop chair, designed by Robin Day for Hille, is truly a modern classic. These daddy, mommy and baby Series E chairs are to be seen practically everywhere you look: schools, town halls, factories, offices. Available in many different forms, over half a million of these molded polypropylene, steel-framed chairs have been made every year since 1962.

In the sphere of furniture, the chair should be viewed as a special case. In essence, it is no more than a simple stool with a backrest, fulfilling the basic human need to rest. It is also an icon—the designer's equivalent of the artist's self-portrait. It is now as feasible to collect contemporary chairs from different designers as it is to collect paintings, the advantage being that a well-designed chair is both beautiful *and* supremely practical.

If designers are willing to put their names to a particular product, either manufactured under their own name or for another company, they must be convinced that the end quality of both the design construction and the finish reflects the values of the brand that they, as leading designers, are wishing to establish. Recognized brand manufacturers such as Cassina and Vitra also play an important role because they realize that their already excellent manufacturing quality can have added value with good innovative design.

There is no doubt that some chain stores offer superb furnishing style at excellent prices. They are able to do this by following trends set by leading designers and expending their efforts on good sourcing and distribution. Leading designers are usually acclaimed for good reason: they produce high-quality, imaginative, original, innovative and usually well-thought-out designs, and these will always have an unmatched intrinsic value.

One thing all furniture has in common is its basic function. The differences occur in the quality of design, attention to detail, materials and manufacture. Not all designs provide the same solutions to a functional requirement. As an example, dining chairs can have different forms, materials, numbers of legs, finishes, back details, cost and so on, but they all tend to be made to the same height to suit the average human form.

When choosing furniture, always first look at the very best (even if it is out of your price range), as this orients the mind, allowing you to judge the merits of more affordable pieces. Save up for a piece you want—it is worth the wait and sacrifice.

What differentiates modern living from yesterday's traditions is the need to make the best use of space, an impact of new technology and social change. A good example is the trend toward open-plan style—the advent of the kitchen/dining/living room is due to a combination of improved draft exclusion and heating methods and the introduction of labor- and space-saving devices, such as dishwashers and modular construction techniques.

The need or desire to work from home has meant that the spare bedroom or a corner of the living room may now double as a home office. The result is that we need to get the maximum function out of our furniture—a sofa becomes a bed for occasional guests, daytime work equipment and papers may need to be hidden from view in the evening, a dining table doubles as a desk.

Leading designers are usually acclaimed for good reason: they produce high-quality, innovative, original, practical, imaginative and usually well-thought-out designs.

the DNA of the chair

1900
charles rennie mackintosh

Modernist furniture design really began in 1918 with Dutch architect Gerrit Rietveld and the floating lines of his *Red/Blue Chair,* although in the nineteenth century Scots architect Charles Rennie Mackintosh played an important stylistic role and Michael Thonet pioneered industrial manufacturing. In the 1920s, Eileen Gray and Le Corbusier designed furniture to complement their Modernist buildings using new industrial processes. In pre-Nazi Germany, at the famous Bauhaus design school, Marcel Breuer designed the sling-seated chair for artist Kandinsky and the cantilevered *Cesa* chair, aimed at industrial manufacture. In 1930s Finland, Alvar Aalto explored the possibilities of using the simple curves of molded plywood to give unique forms. In the 1940s, the American designers Charles Eames and George Nelson used plywood and new materials such as reinforced plastics. During the 1950s, Europe emerged from post-war hibernation and Italian Gió Ponti designed the elegant *Superleggera* chair, one of many innovative Italian designs. With the advent of air travel and digital communications, design has become truly global and no longer relies on local centers of excellence.

1859
michael thonet

1918
gerrit rietveld

1925
marcel breuer

1928
marcel breuer

1929
ludwig mies van der rohe

1930
alvar aalto

1934
gerrit rietveld

1952
gió ponti

1956
eero saarinen

1957
arne jacobsen

1959
verner panton

1988
jasper morrison

material choices

material choices

Once there was a time when rare and exotic materials were considered chic. Thankfully, fashions change for the better and it is now about as acceptable to detail a table in teak from endangered rain forests as it is to trim a coat with real leopard fur.

Manufacturing methods have changed too, offering contemporary designers a previously unrivaled range of choices in what they are able to create and the style they can achieve. As technology improves, so do materials. Plastics, for instance, once shunned as being "cheap and nasty," have become more stable and have gained a deserved acceptability.

The materials used in contemporary furniture vary tremendously, from the naturally found (such as wood, leather and most textiles) to the industrially produced (such as steel, glass and plastics). The materials chosen have a profound effect on the form, style and feel of the furniture composed from them and are often the dominant characteristic in the coordination and theming of a living space. Of the many considerations a designer takes into account when choosing materials and their suitability, the primary ones are their physical strength, appearance, workability and cost.

Never before has the furniture designer had so many materials and industrial processes to choose from. Cross-fertilization is also at work. Complex technology created for the aerospace industry is finding its way into furniture very quickly, and the growing use of space-age technology materials, such as Kevlar, carbon fiber and composite laminates, gives strength and lightness to the pieces created. And there is always the desire of designers to make their mark by being the first to embrace the emerging technologies.

The Wiggle Side Chair, designed by Frank O. Gehry for Vitra in 1972 and made of laminated, recycled cardboard, is an interesting experiment in transferring packaging technology to furniture. The innate strength and volume of the corrugated cardboard gives this piece improbable structural integrity with surprising comfort.

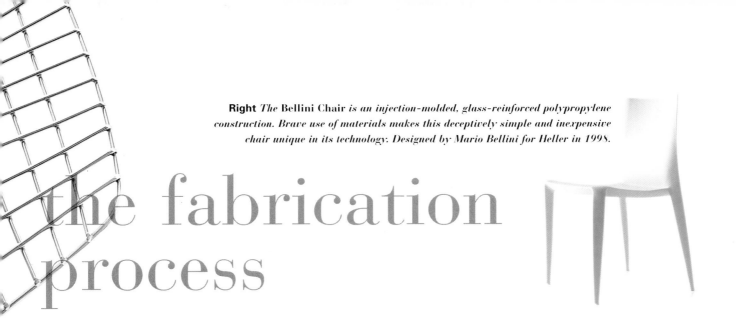

Right *The Bellini Chair is an injection-molded, glass-reinforced polypropylene construction. Brave use of materials makes this deceptively simple and inexpensive chair unique in its technology. Designed by Mario Bellini for Heller in 1998.*

the fabrication process

The essential difference of modern furniture from that of the past is that, with few exceptions, contemporary furniture is manufactured using industrial processes whereas in the past furniture was fashioned by craftsmen using traditional skills.

Industrialization of the furniture industry grew throughout the eighteenth and nineteenth centuries. In Austria in 1856, Michael Thonet was the first to use true industrial process to make furniture. He met the demand for inexpensive, light and durable restaurant and café furniture with his new patented process based on his discovery that beech-wood rails became flexible when heated in steam ovens—almost like rubber hose—only to become rigid again when they cooled. Over forty million of the functional but elegant *Type 14* chairs (see page 20) were manufactured between 1860 and the First World War. These were mainly used to supply the new vogue for Viennese coffeehouses.

Furniture is now manufactured using hundreds of processes. Newly developed materials and processes such as injection-molded engineering plastics and extruded aluminum are now commonplace. This has had a dramatic effect on the materials used, the subsequent design options and, therefore, the furniture's appearance. Craft-based techniques commonplace in the workshop of old are now too uneconomical to be widely used.

Previously undreamed-of forms are now available to the designer who can construct a virtual model of his creation in the ether of a computer and view it on screen. This has the benefits of reducing the costs of repeated prototypes and improving timescale but, perhaps more importantly, it allows designers to create and visualize something that once could only be imagined.

Even if some functional aspects of furniture have changed to incorporate modern technology requirements such as the television and computer, human proportions still remain pretty similar and the basic needs of work-eat-relax-sleep remain the same.

Left *Designer/sculptor Harry Bertoia's weld-mesh chair is almost transparent to light and air, causing no shadows and little impact on the space around it. Diamond Chair was designed for Knoll International in 1950–52.*

wood

Wood is the traditional material for furniture. Whether it is sawn, carved, turned or laminated, wood provides furniture with natural appeal. Used judiciously, wood has the advantage of being tough, light and decorative. It is no coincidence that the fastest and one of the most successful airplanes of the Second World War was the plywood-constructed Mosquito, utilizing Britain's furniture workshops.

The woods used today mainly come from sustainable, farmed sources where the act of growing absorbs carbon dioxide from the atmosphere, thus cleansing the air. This makes it one of the most environmentally sound materials. However, rain forest hardwoods can take hundreds of years to grow, so check the origin if in doubt. The appearance and properties of wood can vary tremendously. For example, ash and beech are both pale hardwoods that can be easily steam-bent and are suitable for structural use. They are consistent and relatively plentiful, too—qualities that can lead to industrial uses not available with other woods.

An example of excellent wood engineering is designer Gió Ponti's 1952 dining chair (see page 21). Its triangular ash-wood frame combines the minimum of material with the maximum rigidity, hence its name: *Superleggera* (super-light). To my mind, it is still one of the lightest and most beautiful creations you can sit on.

Above and near left (top) *Frank O. Gehry's* Cross-Check Armchair *(1990–92, for Vitra) has a bent and woven laminated wood construction. These sensuous ribbons of maple owe their conception to Michael Thonet's original manufacturing process.*
Far left (top) and near right (bottom) Chair 471, *designed by Christoph Zschocke in 1992 for Gebrüder Thonet GmbH, is constructed from solid and laminated woods and demonstrates a range of different wood processes including formed laminated plywood and computer-machined forms.*
Far left (bottom) *Charles and Ray Eames's* LCW (Lounge Chair Wood) *dates from 1945. The laminated ash frame and formed plywood seat provide good support and comfort. An early classic designed for the Museum of Modern Art* Organic Design in Home Furnishings *competition, this is still produced by Vitra.*

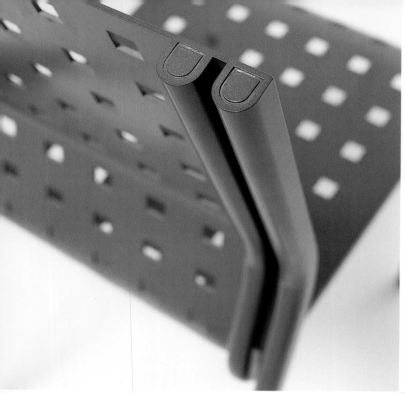

Above and below *Jasper Morrison's* **Thinking Man's Chair,** *designed in 1987 for Cappellini, is made from iron-oxide-painted tubular and flat-bar steel. This chair established Morrison's cerebral approach to tackling design challenges with sophisticated simplicity.*

Above and below *The* **Mirandolina** *chair was designed by Pietro Arosio for Zanotta in 1992. Its aluminum construction is ingeniously formed from a single stamping of a unique extrusion without any welding or hardware; the chair's simplicity belies the sophisticated nature of its construction.*

metal

Right How High the Moon, *Shiro Kuramata's 1986 design for Vitra, is made from nickel-plated expanded metal. The springy feel of this witty take on the archetypal armchair makes it a disconcerting perch. Perhaps more "art" than design?* **Below** Ruhs Panca *is constructed from tube and rod welded together, making this visually delicate, low table-seat an interesting choice. Designed by Kris Ruhs in 1991 for Cappellini.*

Metal has been used in furniture since its first discovery. Although sometimes used decoratively in the past, more often it was used to provide structural reinforcement and functional mechanisms such as locks and hinges. It was the invention of the screw that made metal really useful.

Early examples of metal being used visibly as a principal structural material are typified by cast- or wrought-iron garden furniture. With the advent of industrially produced, cheap tubular steel and chrome plating in the 1920s, a new genre of tubular steel furniture appeared, as in Marcel Breuer's *Cesa* chair of 1928 (see page 21).

Metals fall into one of two categories—ferrous or non-ferrous—depending upon whether they are alloyed with iron. Just like wood, all metals have their individual properties. Steel, an alloy of iron, is the mainstay of furniture; it is strong, cheap and reliable, and can be rolled into strip, tube and sheet. This can then be cut, folded, bent and welded (see *Thinking Man's Chair*, opposite). Steel does corrode easily so it needs to be protected by paint, powder coating or plating if it is to be visible. Many fasteners such as hinges, screws and nails are made from steel.

Bronze, a copper alloy, is one of man's oldest metals. It is quite expensive but easily cast, so it is often used decoratively where its soft brown color adds an aura of quality. Brass and zinc alloys are more affordable.

Aluminum does not corrode indoors. It is light, soft and compliant and can be easily extruded into rails, rolled into sheets and stamped (see *Mirandolina* chair, opposite), spun into dishes, machined from blocks and sand cast or die cast. It is typically used in the star bases of swivel chairs such as the *Aeron* chair (see pages 56–7). Once fearfully expensive, it is now accessible and its use increasingly widespread.

Stainless steel does not necessarily contain iron. There are many types of alloy with varying properties. Generally, they are strong and self-finishing, so stainless steel can be used in thin sections. It has a hard, uncompromising appearance, but it is also malleable and can be finished in many ways, such as brushing or polishing.

plastic

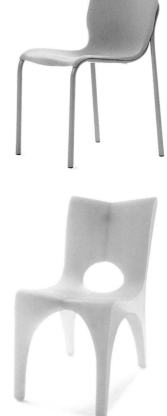

Originally developed as a substitute for horn and ivory, plastic is mankind's first truly synthetic material. As most plastics are derived from crude oil, their use is often criticized for being environmentally insensitive. However, in the majority of designs this is not the case. For example, consider Robin Day's *Series E Polyprop* chair (see page 18). This polypropylene chair seat once might have been a few gallons of gasoline or oil but as a chair it performs a useful service and can be recycled.

Although most plastics come from the same source, there are different types with varying characteristics depending on how they are formed. Fiberglass is a liquid resin reinforced with glass fiber strands and hardened in a mold. When set, it gives a permanent, hard finish on one side that can be self-colored or painted. It is useful in furniture since it is relatively cheap to mold, and size is not a barrier. However, it is expensive since it involves skilled, labor-intensive work, is rather inconsistent and fragile and generally only has one good surface.

Like wax, thermoplastics are heat-formable and can be molded in a variety of ways. Most common are vacuum-forming, rotational molding (see opposite) and injection molding. Injection molding, a process where liquid plastic is injected into a hard steel mold under high pressure, gives a good finish, but the making of large molds can be prohibitively expensive.

Top right Cheap Chic, *designed by Philippe Starck for Xo in 1997, has an injection-molded plastic seat and back and a welded steel tubular frame. Extremely comfortable, practical, inexpensive and (for Starck) uncharacteristically restrained.*

Left and center right Chasm *is a rotational-molded polyethylene chair. This is an innovative solution for economical small batch production runs. Designed by Will White and Katarina Barac at One Foot Taller in 1998 for Nicehouse Limited.*

Bottom right RCP2 Plastic Chair *shows an intriguing use of recycled plastic packaging. Designed in 1992 by Jane Atfield for Made of Waste.*

Above left *The Butterfly Chair, which dates from 1938, comprises slung canvas on a mild steel rod frame. Pictured is a contemporary interpretation of the classic chair, designed by Jorge Ferrari-Hardoy, Juan Kurchan and Antonio Bonet.*

Above right *Nigel Coates's chair from The Slipper Collection 60a for Hitch-Mylius in 1995 has a beech and preformed plywood frame with an upholstered seat. Restrained and elegant, this classic chair quietly fits in with many different decorative styles.*

Below left *The 21 Hotel Grand Suite chair could not be more different from the piece shown above. Its striking colors and jarring forms create a charismatic sculptural form that will dominate most surroundings. Designed by Javier Mariscal in 1997 for Moroso.*

fabric & upholstery

Textiles are easily colored, printed or woven and can soften the appearance of an otherwise severe structure, adding texture and color as well as being soft to the touch. Seating intended for relaxation, such as a sofa or armchair, is an obvious candidate for upholstery to cushion and warm the body.

The fabrics most commonly used are wool, linen and cotton. Wool can be dyed any color, can have a variety of woven textures and patterns, and is fairly stain resistant and hard-wearing. Cotton is less expensive and can have a woven texture, but its best feature is that it is easy to print. However, it is less hard-wearing and stain resistant (unless treated with a protective finish).

Synthetic textiles and blends are being developed with excellent performance and new characteristics such as stretchability, which allows for fewer seams on rounded forms. The techniques of using them are also changing, influenced by mass production methods. A good example is the *Wink* chair, which can adjust its back-to-seat angle and unfold into a reclining lounger (see page 9).

Above *Martin Ryan's Lulu chair, 1997, is available in two sizes. This supremely comfortable dining chair supports the back particularly well.*

Charles and Ray Eames's **Lounge Chair and Ottoman**, *designed in 1956, is an enduring classic. It is one of the most comfortable chairs ever designed, setting new standards of manufacturing technology that are still relevant today. The leather-covered cushions sit on rosewood-faced molded plywood seat shells set on a cast aluminum base.*

leather

Left *Mario Bellini's* **Cab Chair** *has a steel frame with a zipper-fastening, heavy-duty stitched leather covering with integral polyurethane seat cushion. The natural finishing on the bridle leather ensures that this will improve gracefully with age. Designed for Cassina in 1976.*

Alongside wood, leather is one of the oldest materials used by man, although today's soft and colorful leathers scarcely resemble the simple stuff of our early fore-bears.

The laborious and elaborate processes of turning an animal skin into luxurious leather makes it an expensive option for upholstery. There are many types of leather, the best being cow or horse hide. Pigskin and sheepskin nappa are also viable alternatives but less popular due to their smaller size and decreased durability. There are a wide number of finishes, coatings and embossed textures available, the finest for uphol-stery being vat-dyed aniline hide. For more structural uses, such as sling seats, bridle leather can look good, especially if saddle-stitched.

Leather does have almost romantic qualities that no other material can offer—even its lingering fragrance is evocative of the quality of bygone eras. Like wood, it can look even better when aged and battered. It is also very practical—only the uncoated aniline leathers stain.

Below *The* **Balzac Armchair and Ottoman** *was designed by Matthew Hilton for SCP in 1991. This clubby, comfortable chair, with a leather-covered polyurethane foam–upholstered wood frame with American oak legs, works well in many different situations.*

out of the ordinary

Inflatable Chair *has welded inflatable sections with chrome-plated steel tube and wood frame. Space-age and futuristic-looking, Nick Crosbie's chair was designed for Inflate in 1997.*

Designers are always exploring new ways of making furniture using materials and technologies from other industries. These pieces often emanate from small studios where designers take risks that large manufacturers cannot consider. This conceptual approach can lead to provocative pieces that take on icongraphic status. The uncompromising style of their designs often means they are unsuitable for volume production and are made as single, unique pieces or in small batches. This can make them collectable, being used as semi-functional sculpture to give an interesting edge to a room. Opting for innovative furniture may seem to be a risk compared to buying reproductions of classics, but it is worth it to buy originals. Arne Jacobsen's *Ant* chair was innovative and influential in the 1960s and an original is now worth much more than lesser-quality designs inspired by it. It is likely this will also apply to contemporary rising stars.

Ghost *is made from molded, toughened glass—an ingenious one-piece form that is stronger than you might think. This is similar to wire mesh furniture in that it casts no shadow and makes little visual impact on space. Designed by Cino Boeri and Tomu Katayanagi for Fiam in 1987.*

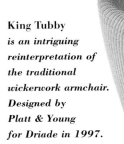

King Tubby *is an intriguing reinterpretation of the traditional wickerwork armchair. Designed by Platt & Young for Driade in 1997.*

Left *Tom Dixon's* S Chair, *designed for Cappellini in 1988, is not the most comfortable of chairs, but is one of the most striking—a visually strong sculptural statement in any space.*

furniture

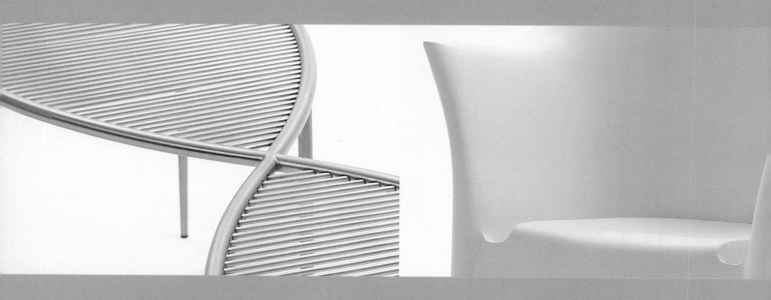

room by room

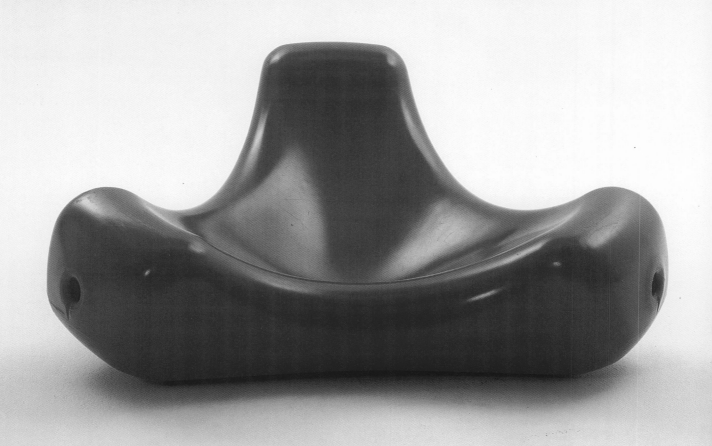

furniture room by room

This chapter leads you through the home room by room, showing you what we consider to be some of the best new designs in furniture, explaining how to get the most from the pieces you choose and giving some indications of current and future trends.

In our selection of furniture, we emphasize strongly the importance of supporting the talent of original furniture designers. We believe that many of the items featured on the following pages are destined to become the classics of the future, and some furniture buyers with fore-sight are already beginning to accumulate pieces by these young designers, believing that they are the collectibles of tomorrow.

Many of the pieces we like most are the physical manifestations of an idea or concept and, as such, have a story to tell. We ask ourselves, were the designers or manufacturers the first to use such a construction method, is the piece an homage to another designer or artist, is its form notable? Since an object without heritage clearly cannot exist, it follows that the richer the history, the more interesting the piece. With art, the smaller the edition, the more valuable the print; with furniture, a unique original will rarely have the refined finesse or provenance of the limited edition, but ubiquity has an inverse relationship to value.

Marc Newson's Bucky, 1997, is made from molded polyethylene and is clearly inspired by the architectural guru Buckminster Fuller's geodesic dome. This chair is based on one of the dome's modules and theoretically, if attached to enough other seats, would form a large sphere.

kitchens

The impact of pre-prepared foods, cleaner cooking technologies and improved air extraction has allowed the kitchen to become a more accommodating environment. This, combined with ever-changing social trends, has helped the kitchen to fast become the new focus of the home. The move away from formality and the tendency toward open-plan kitchen/dining room combinations create larger, more friendly living spaces. The kitchen is no longer a hidden room but the center for family life and a place for informal socializing.

Out of this change comes the need to combine the functions of the food preparation area with informal eating and entertaining. The higher work surface required for good posture while standing and cooking is met by the introduction of tall stools for comfortable seating. Surfaces and finishes come under greater attack in the heat of the kitchen than anywhere else in the home, so durability, scratch endurance, and water and stain resistance are important practical considerations when selecting furniture in this area.

The Atlas Stool, designed by Jasper Morrison for Alias, has a powder-coated steel frame with fabric- or leather-covered polyurethane seats. The swagged bottleneck detail on the seat stem is typical of Morrison's understated attitude.

The bar-height Beatnik High Table, designed by Jonas Lindvall in 1996, with accompanying solid birch, clear-lacquered stools, works for food preparation as well as for eating—ideal for the kitchen or the creative workspace.

Left *Philippe Starck's* **Cheap Chic Bar Stool,** *designed for Xo in 1997, is one of the most comfortable plastic chairs available. It is made from injection-molded plastic with a tubular steel frame. The translucent version of this piece is particularly striking (see dining version on page 33).*

Right Tiramisù, *designed by Andries van Onck for Kartell, is a very useful and stylish kitchen accessory, available in various subdued colors. The molded plastic handle and steps have a tubular steel frame.*

Below right *The* Arion Bar Stool, *from the Terence Conran Collection Design Team, 1997—a laminated beech seat with aluminum tube base— is also available as a dining chair. A fresh take on the traditional Spanish bar stool, the curved timber seat makes for a comfortable perch.*

With modern urban life, space is at a premium and the kitchen is no exception. There is a strong need to maximize whatever space is available, such as with ceiling-height cabinets and shelves. To access these, there are a variety of ingenious solutions, such as lightweight, compact folding steps and more rigid combination stools. Backless stools, although they provide less support, can be usefully stored under work/eating surfaces. High rolling carts have many uses, not only as movable storage for large, cumbersome objects like serving bowls but also to provide an extra surface for food preparation, serving and even dish-washing overload.

As we are now spending more time in the kitchen environment, so the aesthetic design of the essential cooking accessories and other details becomes more evident and more important. Generous cabinet storage is essential for an uncluttered appearance. This is especially important if you do not have the luxury of fully coordinated cooking equipment—but be careful that they don't become a repository for mismatched dishes, junk and never-to-be-used-in-this-lifetime gadgets! The dictum "less is more" applies to the kitchen as much as anywhere else in the home.

Above right Dolly, *designed by Timothy Gadd for Wireworks in 1998, has a powder-coated metal-rod frame, laminated plywood shelves and industrial casters. Useful for small-scale food preparation overflow and storing the odd wok.*

Right *Extend your reach with this practical and elegant fold-away step-stool. Rob Whyte's* Step Stool *for Aero, 1985, has a steel tube and bar construction, coated with silver epoxy.*

dining tables

By tradition, the dining table has been the daily social meeting place for family and friends. Talking over a good meal can be one of life's greatest pleasures. These days, it is rare to find a dining table that is used exclusively for the purpose of dining—more often than not, eating has to fight for precedence over newspapers, magazines, homework and food preparation.

Consideration of these other functions is as important as style and size when choosing. As a rough guide, a table of 35 x 70 inches should comfortably seat six people, or eight at a squeeze. Dining-table legs tend to pose a pretty similar issue—it is worth thinking about human leg space too, especially if you are going to be seating eight regularly.

*Antonio Citterio's Angiolo, designed for B&B Italia in 1996, has a metal frame
with timber top. Also available with an utterly beautiful glass box top.*

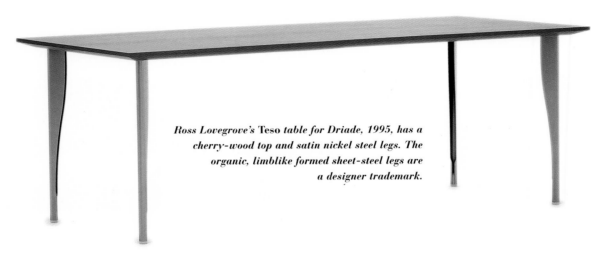

Ross Lovegrove's Teso table for Driade, 1995, has a cherry-wood top and satin nickel steel legs. The organic, limblike formed sheet-steel legs are a designer trademark.

Some people consider natural wood to be the most pleasant surface for dining. Durability of finish and heat- and stain resistance are important too, and these challenges are well met by the many types of laminates now available. Glass surfaces can look stylish, but their transparency can be a little awkward for modest diners. Rectangular tables tend to be the most practical and the best value. Round and oval tables look good—they are

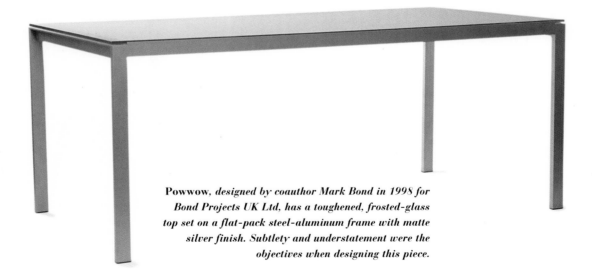

Powwow, designed by coauthor Mark Bond in 1998 for Bond Projects UK Ltd, has a toughened, frosted-glass top set on a flat-pack steel-aluminum frame with matte silver finish. Subtlety and understatement were the objectives when designing this piece.

Simon Pengelly's "V" Table, 1994, has a beech and laminate top. The joints are a particularly satisfying detail on this practical trestlelike table.

also easier to converse around and less cumbersome in a room, although they can be difficult to set, especially the smaller ovals. Do ensure that they are stable, particularly if they have a pedestal base that provides good leg space but less rigidity. Expanding tables with pull-out and hinged leaves can be very useful and are particularly worth considering if the room has space constraints and you expect to be especially social.

Daytona *has folding tubular metal legs and a formed laminate top with a curved lip. Designed by Wiebe Boonstra, Martijn Hoogend and Marc van Nederpel for Dumoffice in 1997–98, it is especially useful for small spaces.*

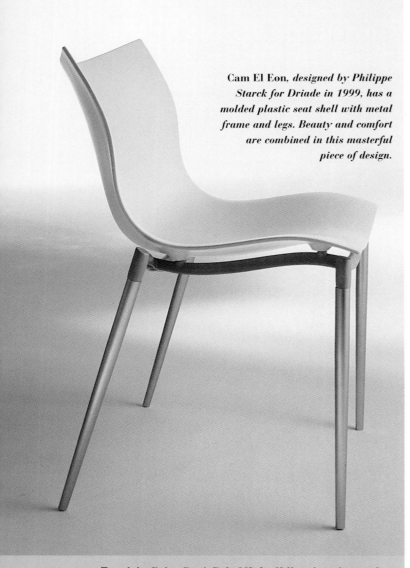

Cam El Eon, *designed by Philippe Starck for Driade in 1999, has a molded plastic seat shell with metal frame and legs. Beauty and comfort are combined in this masterful piece of design.*

Top right *Robin Day's* Polo M5 *for Hille—the polypropylene chair with the holes in it! Advanced for its day, a good value and still chic after over thirty years in production.*
Middle right Dakota, *by Paolo Rizzatto for Cassina, 1995, is futuristically styled in the millennial manner.*
Bottom right *Rob Whyte's 1989 Flower Chair for Aero, made in silver epoxy-covered steel, is visually severe but unobtrusive.*

dining chairs

Above Dolly, *by Antonio Citterio for Kartell, 1998, has a folding structure. Sophisticated with a gazelle-like elegance.*
Below Maui, *by the "maestro" Vico Magistretti for Kartell, is a vertically stacking chair with a plastic molded seat and back on a chrome frame. Comfortable, accessible and extremely beautiful.*

Experience shows that dining chairs can take quite a battering, especially in a family environment. People do lean back, especially when relaxed, and exert quite a force on the rear legs and frame. If this is likely, look for durability as well as style. Some of the more recent chair designs by Vico Magistretti and Philippe Starck, featuring injection-molded plastic seats and metal tube legs, are particularly practical since they are tough, can be stacked and are suitable for summer outdoor use too.

Chairs with arms (or carvers, as they are known) work well at the head of a rectangular table. They can be awkward and cumbersome if the arms cannot slide below the table surface, so it's wise to check dimensions of both the table and the chairs before buying. It is not strictly necessary that all your dining chairs match—in fact it can be quite effective to have your six favorite designers represented around the table. It is, however, important that whatever effect you wish to achieve, it should look deliberate rather than accidental. It is also quite beneficial to consider buying eight chairs even if you only intend to set six around the table. The two spares can usually find useful homes in spare rooms.

Near right *Jasper Morrison's Ply Chair, for Vitra in 1989, has a plywood section with birch-faced veneer. It is a strong, comfortable chair, available with either an open or closed back.*

Near left *Charles and Ray Eames's classic LCW (Lounge Chair Wood), made in 1945 for Vitra. The laminated ash seat and back sit on rubber mounts that allow flexibility, making this a typically comfortable Eames's design.*

Opposite below *Verner Panton's* **Panton Chair,** *made for Vitra in 1959–60, has a mono-component construction. Originally manufactured from fiberglass, it is now also available in less expensive molded polypropylene.*

Right Fantastic Plastic Elastic, *designed by Ron Arad for Kartell in 1999, is inventively fashioned from aluminum extrusions and sheet plastic. The back and seat provides improbable structural stability.*

home office

Aeron, designed by Donald Chadwick and William Stumpf for Herman Miller in 1992, comes in three sizes, has a recycled aluminum and fiberglass-reinforced polyester frame and base with polyester mesh seat. This is our seat of choice—I am sitting on one as I write—it is admittedly eye-wateringly expensive and worth every penny.

As life becomes more complex and computers and digital communications continue to influence the way we work and live, there is an increasing need to work from home.

The most important piece of furniture in any office is the work chair. An ergonomically correct, swiveling chair with an adjustable seat height is essential if you are to be working for any length of time at a computer.

For health, it is also very important to have the screen set at eye level, the keyboard placed at elbow height, your spine straight and your feet firmly supported.

A well-designed work chair is a pleasure to use. By assisting correct posture, it aids concentration and prevents fatigue and back pain. Try many chairs and sit on them for a while to see if they suit you. A good work chair is a sound investment you will never regret.

Left *James Irvine's* **Archiver** *bookcase for SCP is constructed from laminated MDF and is set on a particularly useful swivel base.*
Below Mobil, *designed by Antonio Citterio and Oliver Löw for Kartell, has injection-molded plastic drawers in strong translucent colors and a chrome-plated framework. It is available in several different styles.*

There are a number of well-designed home work-stations now on the market. However stylish they are, they do tend to get a bit lost amid the morass of cables and dull gray boxes. When choosing a desk or a work-station, consider future as well as current equipment requirements. You will need plenty of storage—they may talk of the paperless office but experience seems to suggest quite the opposite! Again, for posture it is important to get an adjustable-height work surface or sliding keyboard shelf. It's useful to have a means of adjusting the computer screen to be level with your eyes. A workstation with casters means you can swing it out if you need to get to the back of the equipment.

Below left *Monica Armani's* **Project 1** *table is made from steel with a veneered birch drawer unit. This system incorporates various functions as well as different materials and finishes. The ingenious details are subtle and sophisticated.*
Below right *Bisley's ubiquitous filing system unit is available in interesting colors and finishes, making it more domestically suitable.*

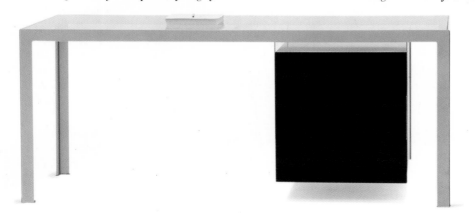 

Above *The* Meda Chair, *by Alberto Meda for Vitra, 1997, is a swivel chair on a five-star base with casters, with or without armrests. Quieter in appearance than the Aeron on page 56, this chair nonetheless offers a lot of the same excellent features in a less macho package.*

Right *Arne Jacobsen's* Series 7 Model No. 3217, *designed for Fritz Hansen in 1955, is a molded plywood seat with a seat pad, set on a height-adjustable chromed tubular steel frame with double-wheel casters. Although classic in its look, this chair does not have the benefit of the last forty years of ergonomic technological progress.*

Above *The* Juli Chair, *by Werner Aisslinger for Cappellini, 1996, is a self-upholstered foam seat shell on a height-adjustable five-star base with casters. More domestic-looking than most office-use-designed furniture.*

sofas

A large, comfortable sofa is a wonderful thing to come home to, to snuggle up on in front of a romantic movie or to settle in with the Sunday paper on a rainy afternoon. It can also make a useful yet conveniently not-too-comfortable spare bed when that distant relative comes to stay!

For more formal social interaction, two smaller sofas separated by a low table are often better than one large one. If you have a beautiful rug or an elegant wooden floor, a higher sofa set on legs allows light to filter through effectively—it's also more practical for cleaning underneath and for crawling children, too.

Sofas can dominate an environment both physically and visually so the choice of design and fabric have to be well considered, taking into account room circulation and aesthetic ambience.

The most important question to ask when choosing a sofa is "Can I get it into the room?" It is amazing how much large furniture is squeezed through front doors, only to be shipwrecked on the first landing. Frustrating, expensive . . . in short, heartbreaking. So it is wise to check whether a sofa can be disassembled and to go shopping with a measured room plan, including door and window sizes.

The Stafford Sofa has a molded glass-reinforced plastic shell, inlaid with foam and topped with removable covers, and American oak legs. Andrew Stafford's 1998 sofa for SCP is practical and comfortable (in an upright sort of way). An innovative mix of materials gives a light, airy look.

Opposite above *Jasper Morrison's* Sofa *for SCP, 1988, is classically styled with subtle details. This tall piece is more comfortable than its austere lines convey. It has a beech frame with multidensity foam, a feather cushion and aluminum feet.*

Opposite below *The* Woodgate Modular Sofa System *provides a very practical seating solution, if a little severe and low looking. Designed by Terence Woodgate for SCP in 1997, it has a beech frame with feather or foam cushions and stainless steel legs. The matching table completes the corner of the rectangle or square in a pleasing manner.*

Matthew Hilton's Balzac Sofa *for SCP, 1991, has a beech frame with multidensity foam, feather cushions and American oak legs. Visually opulent in the traditional manner. (See page 37 for matching armchair and ottoman—an ideal take on the three-piece suite.)*

A large, comfortable sofa is a wonderful thing to come home to.

George Nelson's Coconut Chair, *designed in 1955, has a seat of reinforced white fiberglass plastic, chromed steel base and one-piece leather upholstery. This looks like a design of tomorrow rather than one of more than forty years ago. Although relatively obscure for some time, George Nelson is proving to be quite an inspiration to some leading contemporary designers.*

easy
chairs

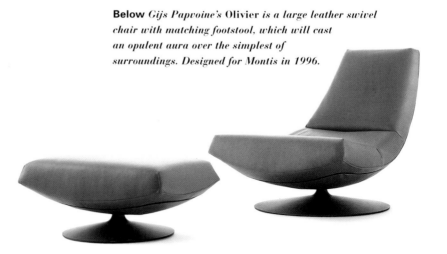

Below *Gijs Papvoine's* Olivier *is a large leather swivel chair with matching footstool, which will cast an opulent aura over the simplest of surroundings. Designed for Montis in 1996.*

A pair of comfortable easy chairs can often work more effectively in a room than a two-seater sofa that modest types might not want to share. Separate chairs also have the distinct benefit of being much easier to arrange and rearrange later if you need functional flexibility in your room. The chairs featured on these pages would work well individually in most room settings, whatever their style.

A comfortable swiveling and reclining chair, positioned near good light or by a window with an ottoman, provides one of the best ways to enjoy a quiet afternoon with a good book.

Far left Y's Chair, *by Christophe Pillet for Cappellini in 1995, is a polyurethane foam seat shell on swiveling cast-aluminum base. Soft to touch and very simple, this chair epitomizes contemporary furniture attitudes.*

Left *The compact and extremely comfortable* Swan Chair *was designed by Arne Jacobsen for Fritz Hansen in 1957–58. It is a fabric-covered, foam-upholstered molded fiberglass seat shell on a swiveling cast-aluminum base. Designed by a master, its classic looks are as relevant today as they ever were.*

If there is enough space around them, large lounge chairs and chaise-longue recliners can offer a good opportunity to make a strong visual statement, setting the scene for the rest of the environment. This is especially so if they are as dramatic and sculptural as are these classic pieces created by Charles Eames and Arne Jacobsen. Although both are well over forty years old, these designs still have a powerfully contemporary aesthetic, which is only betrayed by their period bases.

A lounger can become a favorite friend that welcomes you home after a long day or a tiring journey.

Right The Egg Chair, by Arne Jacobsen for Fritz Hansen, 1957–58, is a definitive icon of 1950s furniture design. It has been used in the set design of many movies, from the James Bond films to 2001: A Space Odyssey. It has a fabric-covered, foam-upholstered molded fiberglass seat shell on a swiveling cast aluminum base with loose seat cushion.

Above La Chaise, by Charles and Ray Eames, is a fiberglass seat shell on a wood and rod base. Although not originally put into production, this amoebic-shaped chair seems to be inspired by the work of then-contemporary sculptor Henry Moore. Without moving parts, the form gives a choice of several positions, from reclined to upright. Designed in 1948, it is now made by Vitra.

other seating

When shopping for furniture for relaxing, don't limit yourself to sofas and easy chairs—there's a good range of alternatives now available from leading designers. Super-sized floor cushions can be fun and are especially useful if you have children, since the cushions sit below your sight line in front of the television. However, they are very informal and do become progressively more difficult to use as one ages, so don't expect your older

visitors to relish them. It is worth pointing out that they do draw attention to the floor covering and its condition; also, sitting on them can be fairly isolating if the rest of the furniture is not at the same height. Low-level daybeds can work well with floor cushions, positioned both at the edge and in the center of a room.

Left Tato *and* Tatone *are foam-filled floor stools upholstered in a nylon knit. Available in several shapes and colors, these pieces are actually quite supportive and firm to sit on, making useful perches. Designed by Enrico Baleri and Denis Santachiara for Baleri Italia in 1995.*

Above Sacco *was designed by Piero Gatti, Cesare Paolini and Franco Teodoro in 1968–69 for Zanotta. This anatomical easy chair is really an oversized envelope containing polystyrene pellets. Often referred to as a "sag bag," this versatile and extremely comfortable floor cushion conforms to and supports your own natural shape—the ideal accompaniment to a Playstation.*

Left Michael Marriott's Missed *daybed, designed for SCP in 1997, is made from a beech frame with multidensity foam and stainless steel legs. Seemingly paying homage to Mies van der Rohe's work, the final effect is refined for more straightforward manufacturing methods.*

side tables

Side tables and the ubiquitous "coffee tables" are quite essential partners to the sofa, not only for displaying stylish art books and table lamps, but also for resting the more mundane mug of coffee and remote control for the television. Tables with some space for storage underneath can be very useful to give a tidy look to the room. Glass-topped tables are good for letting light through and giving a sense of space, as well as for setting on patterned rugs; do be careful if using glass or sharp-edged tables with young children around.

Above left *James Irvine's* Fly Table, *for Cappellini, 1995, has a colored glass top on tubular metal framework. Available with many different glass colors, shapes and sizes—chic and simple.*

Below *The* Loop Table *is made from plywood. Ample storage space under a low table surface makes this stylish piece particularly useful. Designed by Barber Osgerby Associates for Cappellini in 1997.*

Above Tris *was designed by Antonio Citterio and Oliver Löw for Kartell, 1995–96. The colored plastic tops are set on plain metal legs. Clever and versatile, near-identical nesting tables are useful in many different space-saving situations.*

storage & display

There are those things that you collect through life that you want to see around you, as much for reminiscing as for decorating. Special and significant things from the past, art objects, perhaps gifts—they often need to be displayed, and in a way that enhances a space rather than clutters it. There is also the need to store things like books, CDs and various bits of equipment, like telephones, that need to be easily accessible. Shelves and cabinets can be very useful here, providing hidden and open access. Shelf units such as Jasper Morrison's *B.B. Bookcase* (shown opposite) can also function well as room dividers if you need to partition off a space.

Below Systemi *has a lacquered timber carcass with a chromed steel understructure. This immaculately finished piece is one of a systemized line of forbiddingly rectangular cabinets. Designed in 1996 by Piero Lissoni, manufactured by Cappellini.*

Opposite B.B. Bookcase *is made from lacquered MDF and set on casters. Squaring the circle, this is good for storage, display and as a movable room divider. Designed by Jasper Morrison in 1994, manufactured by Cappellini.*

Below Blister Storage System *has a wood composition body with metallic gray melamine finish and polypropylene doors in three colors. These are especially effective if used as multiples along a wall or as space dividers. Designed by Platt & Young in 1996 and manufactured by Driade.*

Most shelves and cabinets are designed to fit against or attach to the wall. Industrial designer Dieter Rams's seminal *606 Universal Shelving System,* designed for Vitsoe, is flexible, well-thought-out and still contemporary (see below). If you intend to install a wall-mounted shelf-storage like this, make sure the wall is strong enough to take the weight—it is preferable to fix it to an exterior or reinforced wall. Shelves can look great when they are well ordered and not too untidy, and designs with integrated closing cabinets work particularly well.

Tall cabinets with doors like Platt & Young's *Blister Storage System* are a practical way of removing clutter from view—for that fashionable minimalist look, the contoured front detail adds visual interest to an environment. However, they can become repositories for useless junk and they will also consume a lot of visual space in a small room. They provide particularly useful storage if you need the same room to function as a living room, home office or bedroom. Short sideboards are effective and easy to use, especially in smaller rooms; the openness of their construction does not impact too badly on confined spaces.

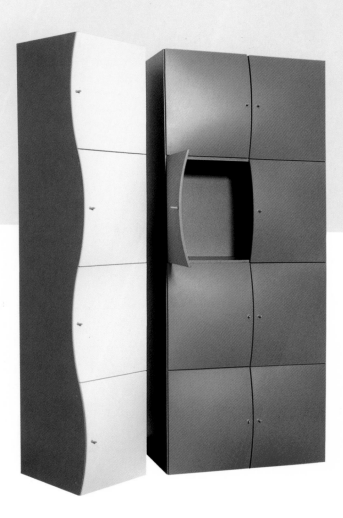

Right 606 Universal Shelving System *is an innovatively constructed system of shelves and storage. Designed in 1960 by Dieter Rams, the master of logical design, it still looks clean and fresh. Manufactured by Vitsoe.*

Above Matrjoska II Cabinet *has shaped layers of plywood with tubular steel legs. An interesting use of plywood with the lamination grain is emphasized as a principal part of the aesthetic. Designed by Olgoj Chorchoj in 1997.*

Left PAB System *is a well-thought-out and exquisitely engineered system of shelf and storage solutions. Designed by Studio Kairos in 1996 and manufactured by B&B Italia.*

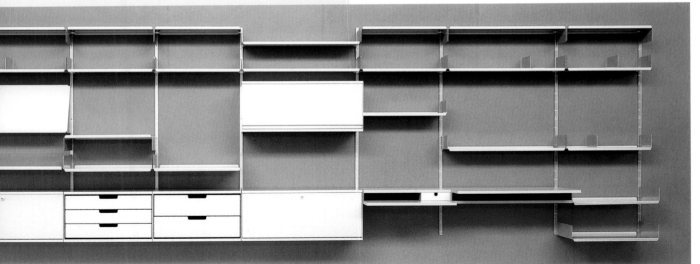

bedrooms

Bedrooms often are neglected, as they are hidden from the view of visitors. It is, however, the room where you spend most of your life, albeit asleep. Not only do you need somewhere to store clothes and linens, but also somewhere to dress and put discarded clothes. That spare dining chair or a simple bench (pictured below) is useful here, as is an armchair or lounger, which would also perform this function well.

As for the bed...consider that you will be using this more than any other piece of furniture in your home, save perhaps a work chair. It is worth getting a really good mattress and as big a bed as is practical. The bed shown here, designed by Andrew Stafford, is particularly good since it has independent back supports that are useful for late-night reading.

Right Bedfordshire *has a molded maple veneer, adjustable headboard and a solid maple frame with sprung beech slats. Designed and manufactured by Andrew Stafford in 1998.*

Left *Alvar Aalto's* 153B Bench *is made from bent and solid birch. It is manufactured by Artek.*

Left *The Atlante wardrobe is made from satin-finish aluminum with white or blue plate-glass finish and frame edges in matte anodized aluminum. Designed by Studio Kairos in 1997 and manufactured by B&B Italia.*

Below *The 90D Stool/Bedside Table, designed by Alvar Aalto in 1930–33, is made from birch-faced plywood with a laminated top. Its compact design makes it ideal for the bedroom.*

The argument for having fewer clothes is a compelling one—a wardrobe with a few favorite items in it is a joy to go to every morning, whereas a bulging mess makes a bad start to the day. It is often a good strategy to be ruthless. Admittedly, clothes are expensive, but ask yourself: Just how many pairs of tatty gardening shoes do I need? And tell me, how do you intend to get your waistline back to that halcyon size? An alternative option is to store out-of-season clothes in another room and change over as appropriate.

The elegant *Atlante* system (pictured opposite) is particularly ingenious and well-thought-out. It provides flexible interior storage combined with sliding doors for maximum space efficiency.

On a practical note, it is useful to have bedroom storage that incorporates different types and sizes of drawers, hanging rails and shelves. A dressing table is also worthwhile: the *Alice,* which includes a full-length mirror and stool, adds a stylish accent to any bedroom. Alternatively, a floor-standing cheval dressing mirror can also be a practical addition.

A wardrobe containing a few favorite items is a joy to use.

Right *Alice dressing table and stool, designed by Matthew Hilton in 1998, is manufactured by SCP. It has a steel frame with solid and veneered walnut drawer unit, a useful velvet-lined jewelry compartment and a mirror.*

outdoors

Left *Philippe Starck's Lord Yo is a stacking polypropylene chair with an aluminum frame. Manufactured by Driade.*

Right *Wire Frame Chair and Stool, designed by Shin and Tomoko Azumi in 1998, is multifunctional and stackable.*

Weather permitting, it's great to be able to get out on a balcony or in the garden to enjoy the breeze and the sky, commune with nature, relax and entertain with some open-air cooking. Although there is no shortage of horrendous outdoor furniture (typified by garish floral vinyl cushions on white plastic) on the market, there are also some excellent pieces of well-considered contemporary furniture.

There are several designs available that work equally well indoors as they do out. Philippe Starck's *Lord Yo* chair is a practical and affordable option that also stacks and works extremely well around an indoor table. It has an elegant style, almost evocative of traditional wicker furniture, combined with the practicality and durability of injection-molded polypropylene. Lounge chairs provide a relaxing way to enjoy the outdoors. Shin and Tomoko Azumi's chair and stool, made with shopping-cart technology, are simple and flexible; the stool works as a side table, and they stack well too.

Above *Armframe, Alberto Meda's 1996 design, has a polished cast-aluminum frame with nylon-mesh seating section. Elegant engineering chic at its most refined. Manufactured by Alias.*

Right *Richard Schultz's* **Leisure Collection Sun Lounger,** *designed in 1966 for B&B Italia, has a cast-aluminum frame and woven-mesh seat sections. One of the original modern garden furniture designs, still looking good after thirty years.*

multifunctional

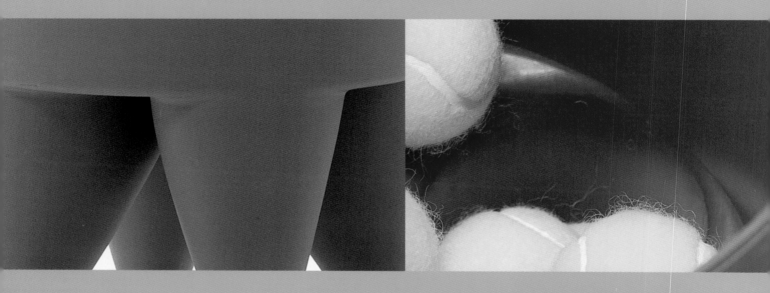

furniture

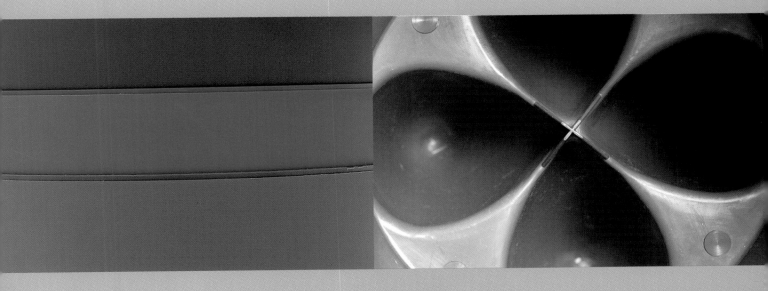

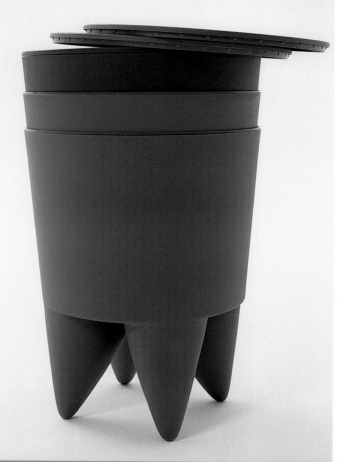

seating
& storage

One commonality of modern life, especially in urban environments, is that living space is at a premium. The result of this is that we often need to maximize precious space by using furniture to perform more than one role. This can often be achieved by simple and ingenious design solutions, where a piece can deliver a number of functions without compromising the different uses.

Storage is particularly hungry for space and in a compact home this can pose quite a few problems if you want it to appear calm and tidy. The simple, time-honored solution is to double up on the function of the piece; for example, as shown here, a storage bin becomes a stool.

Philippe Starck's Bubu is a versatile and colorful low-level, lidded stool-bin, which can serve as bedside table, laundry basket, vegetable bin... in fact, whatever you want. And should you ever run out of uses for them, they can be stacked away. Made from injection-molded polypropylene and manufactured by Xo.

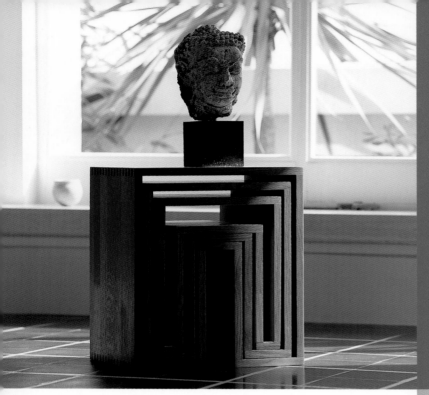

Nesting Tables, designed by Ou Baholyodhin and manufactured by Function. They work as a neat nest of three side tables, act as ad hoc seating with a cushion perched on top, and serve as a stacked display unit. They ably demonstrate how an environment can be easily transformed by moving and arranging a few pieces depending on functional use and entertainment requirements.

storage & display

In many households the same space needs to be used for different purposes, such as living, working and entertaining. This requires furniture that can be used in a variety of ways. Disarmingly simple in their versatility, these elegant nesting seating/storage/display units were designed by Ou Baholyodhin. Perhaps inspired by urban architecture, they seem to reflect the cheek-by-jowl three-dimensional environment of the metropolis. Their open forms allow light to filter through the natural wood, increasing the sense of open space.

technology

Although we crave simplicity, technology can seem to have brought complexity rather than the promised better quality of life. Modern lifestyles are getting to be dominated by supposedly essential gadgetry that is upping the pace of our self-expectations. The problems posed by the burgeoning plethora of imposing electronic equipment, from video recorders and televisions to computers, printers, and their attendant cabling, are difficult to resolve with conventional desk furniture. These challenges are met in a variety of ways, ranging from small, movable, versatile carts to fixed shelving systems like Dieter Rams's *606 Universal Shelving System* (see page 75) and the *Refolo* tech-carts shown here. These work well in many different ways depending on the equipment and usage required.

Konstantin Grcic's Refolo cart, designed for Driade in 1995, has a steel frame painted aluminum gray and a sheet steel top in brick red. It is available in six function versions with color-coded shelves for different uses, such as housing televisions, computers, stereos, etc. There are a variety of add-on functional accessories such as drawers and shelves that allow the carts to be used in other situations, including kitchens and bedrooms.

sleeping

If you haven't got the luxury of a spare room, the occasional need to put someone up overnight or to sleep separately is often best addressed with a sofa bed. These time-honored, space-saving devices range from complex concertina mechanisms that fold out into double beds in an ingenious and improbable manner to simple solutions requiring only folding down armrests and the removal of cushions. Once poorly considered from a comfort point of view, sofa bed mechanisms have become so sophisticated that they are now quite user-friendly—and comfortable enough to use on a nightly basis. Some sofa beds have space for bed linens and can be folded partially made up. When they are folded they are difficult to distinguish from a regular sofa. This makes them ideal if you live in a single-room studio flat.

The advantage of the simpler extending arm solution is that the fold-out leaves can often be used as perch seating, turning a stylish conventional sofa into a chaise longue. This is particularly useful when you have many visitors to host and need to stretch your seating arrangements. They also tend to be more straightforward to use and, in sofa mode, more comfortable and less compromised than the concertina type. They are generally only acceptable as single beds and are not as practical for everyday sleeping. Even if they are a little more expensive than conventional sofas, they are probably a wise choice for the extra flexibility offered.

Jason was designed by Eoos Design for Walter Knoll. It has fabric-upholstered seat cushions and body and removable back and side cushions; the legs are satin matte chrome–plated throughout. This is a good example of the modern approach to a convertible sofa.

versatile working

For people working from home, a common issue is the need to double up the use of the dining table as a desk. The main challenge is to find a way to clear away and store the clutter of the day's work quickly, so that the work does not prey on your mind while relaxing. This can be achieved with a sideboard-style cart that can be swiftly wheeled out of sight.

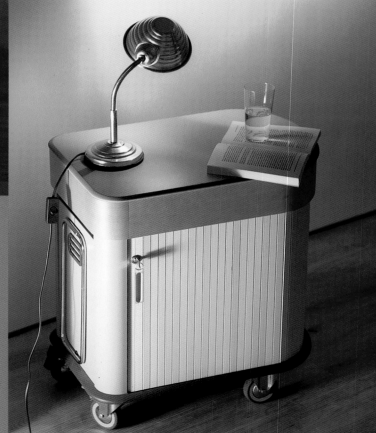

Pearson & Lloyd's Homer *is a portable office. The side table cart with shuttered sides, swiveling top surface and upper storage space is made from a variety of materials, including extruded aluminum, molded plastic and formed plywood. Manufactured by Knoll International in 1999.*

room effects

Buying furniture is the easy part; choosing what is right for your home and arranging it to the best advantage is where it gets complicated. It's comparatively easy to make a large space look good, whereas a small space offers far greater challenges. The golden rule is this: Design the room for yourself and not for other people's eyes. It is your home and you should feel comfortable in it.

The way you use furniture, lighting and color will affect the apparent space of a room dramatically. As a general rule, using low furniture and lights will make a room look bigger; and, of course, the opposite is true of tall furniture and bright lights.

The low table in this room acts centripetally, in almost a campfire-like way, drawing social interaction across it. The large picture window provides a spectacular city view and gives a wall-centric focus to the room. A large painting or a fireplace would act in the same way.

Try not to arrange furniture right up against walls. Where possible, allow space so that light can spill behind and under pieces to give an airy effect. This is more easily achieved if you have upholstered furniture with legs.

Hard finishes and colors can be especially effective against a neutral setting, with wall-to-wall-carpeted floor and plain walls providing uninterrupted lines, setting off the sculptural, severe edges of the furniture. Carpet can also give a warmer, quieter ambience than bare floors,

contrasting with hard surfaces and accommodating the floor cushions well. Here the pale wood of the small stools and the wickerwork lamp help to introduce a more natural element to the room.

Terence Woodgate's L-shaped sofa defines the main seating area and is an eminently practical solution around the custom-designed low coffee table, completing the visual square. It's important with this minimal look to give the individual pieces room to flourish and not to have too much clutter.

Harry Bertoia's classic chromed wire weld-mesh *Diamond* chair appears almost transparent to light, causing no shadows and having very little visual impact on the space it occupies. Charles and Ray Eames's dining chairs with leather cushions produce a similar effect and complement the simple pedestal dining table designed to go with them.

Tom Dixon's rotationally molded *Jack* lights work well singly and in stacked multiples, giving a soft glow at night. By day they have a translucent luminescence when on and a solid sculptural presence when off. Illuminating pale walls from a low level allows the light to reflect off the walls onto the ceiling and into the room, creating the effect of a high ceiling with soft shadows.

A fashionable flooring solution is the ubiquitous hardwood strip. Used with rugs and soft furnishings, it gives a natural, soft look. However, it does feel colder than carpet and reflects and transmits sound (particularly to the apartment below it!). It's practical in that it doesn't stain in the way carpet does, which makes it a good choice in the kitchen or dining room, but be aware that it does scratch easily, especially if your furniture has sharp feet or missing foot ferrules, and it can warp horribly if allowed to get wet.

Continuous flooring can link two adjoining rooms. Here kitchen and dining/living room merge seamlessly. The furniture has been carefully chosen for this effect— the hard-edged steel theme of the kitchen is continued in the choice of table, while the round-edged dining chairs link with the seating used at the far end of the room.

**Big ideas can
enhance the most
unlikely of
small spaces.**

White walls are effective at maximizing the available light and increasing the sense of space. Here the wide wooden shelf softens the otherwise sterile effect that white can create.

This ingenious small-scale micro-workspace has been created in the space above a landing at the top of a flight of stairs. The translucent glass floor and staircase allow daylight to flood in from windows above and below the platform. The neat, translucent white polyethylene *Chasm* chair, together with the small wire-trussed workstation, enhances the overall sense of space and airiness. The directional spotlights playing on the bookcase combine with the work-light in the evening for a dramatic look.

**The bedroom
is the one room
in the house
you can design
with only yourself
in mind.**

You spend more time in the bedroom than in any other room in the house, so it is important to get it right. Your bedroom is what you wake up to each morning, and has the power to color the day ahead; it is preferable to have a soft, calm environment to ease you gently into the day.

The pale wood of the furniture blends well with the blond hardwood floor of this compact bedroom, increasing the sense of space. Subdued walls, bed linens and window blinds continue the theme. Matthew Hilton's minimalist dressing and makeup table usefully combines a full-height tilting mirror with drawers and a matching stool.

The reclining chair provides a secluded retreat for peaceful reading, as well as a useful spot for discarded clothes. A low-level bench placed at the foot of the bed also acts as short-term storage.

Bright sunlight can give harsh shadows that change with the weather, the seasons and the time of day, coloring and softening the look of the garden, terrace or balcony.

Here the white ocean-liner-style reclining lounge chairs, together with the weathered hardwood duckboarding, result in a distinctly nautical ambience. Panoramic glass windows and matching walls allow the inside of the apartment to blend almost seamlessly with the outside. This is also helped by the ceramic tiled floor that permits the same geometric outdoor furniture to be used inside and out, depending on the weather. This spartan approach is a frequent trademark of early classic modernism.

contemporary

designers

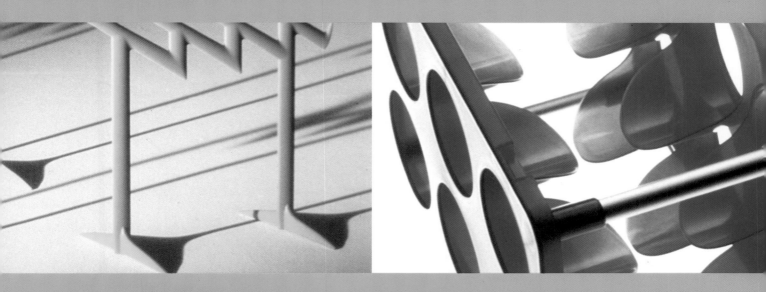

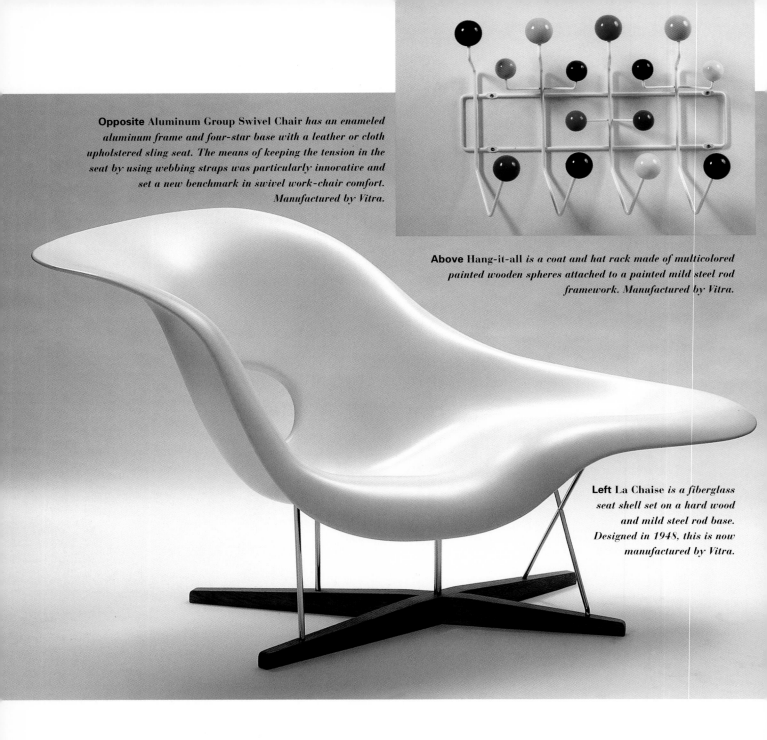

Opposite Aluminum Group Swivel Chair *has an enameled aluminum frame and four-star base with a leather or cloth upholstered sling seat. The means of keeping the tension in the seat by using webbing straps was particularly innovative and set a new benchmark in swivel work-chair comfort. Manufactured by Vitra.*

Above Hang-it-all *is a coat and hat rack made of multicolored painted wooden spheres attached to a painted mild steel rod framework. Manufactured by Vitra.*

Left La Chaise *is a fiberglass seat shell set on a hard wood and mild steel rod base. Designed in 1948, this is now manufactured by Vitra.*

charles & ray eames

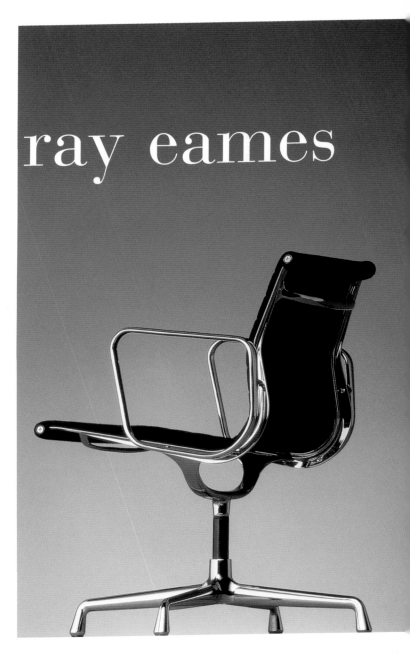

Charles Eames is considered one of the most important founders of "modern" industrially produced furniture. He was born in 1907 and, with his wife Ray, formed a pioneering design partnership that was to have a profound influence on contemporary furniture worldwide.

The Eamses were famed chiefly for their innovative designs for Michigan furniture company Herman Miller. Based in California, they pioneered new technology and materials such as pressed steel, welded wire, fiberglass-reinforced plastics and molded plywood. This led to innovative manufacturing processes as well as unusual organic forms. The Eameses originally started exploring the use of molded plywood with Eero Saarinen (see

Tulip chair, page 21). Fiberglass-reinforced plastic had only been used in aircraft production until the Eameses came across it in a war surplus store. This new material suited the organic forms they were working on. Although Charles died in 1978, his designs continue to be popular and are still in production.

antonio citterio

After graduating as an architect in Milan, Citterio started his design practice in 1972 and was joined by senior partner Terry Dwan from 1987 to 1995. They have worked on a large number of commercial environmental projects, designing factories, offices and shops throughout Europe, the U.S. and Japan.

Citterio has always worked prolifically as an industrial design consultant as well, and has also designed furniture for many notable manufacturers, including B&B Italia, Flos, Kartell and Vitra (for whom he also designed showrooms and a factory). Although not a natural self-publicist, he has quietly created a truly prodigious output and is probably best known for his soft furnishings and influential office furniture.

He has a marked reputation for being able to produce highly marketable, commercial designs. His work is usually technically innovative and is exemplified by its ingenuity, functional efficiency, quiet elegance and the superb attention to detail.

Left *The stackable* **Minni Chair** *has an injection-molded plastic back and seat with legs and arms in solid beech wood. Manufactured by Halifax.*

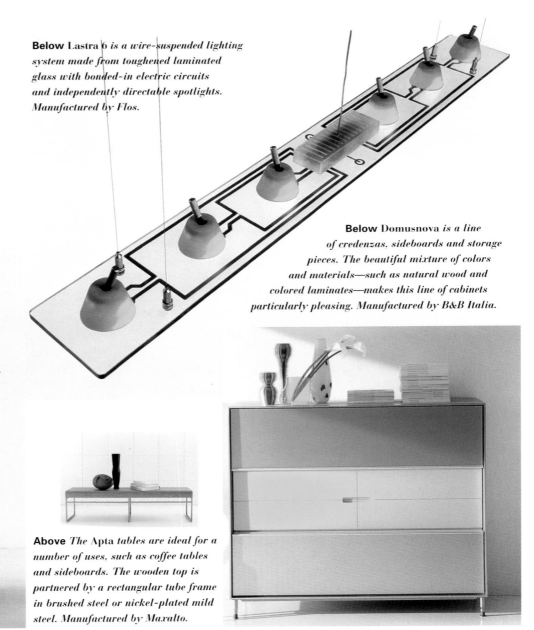

Below Lastra 6 *is a wire-suspended lighting system made from toughened laminated glass with bonded-in electric circuits and independently directable spotlights. Manufactured by Flos.*

Below Charles *is an extremely comfortable, well-made and flexible sofa system. The excellent proportions and refined look allow this to work well in a variety of situations. Manufactured by B&B Italia.*

Below Domusnova *is a line of credenzas, sideboards and storage pieces. The beautiful mixture of colors and materials—such as natural wood and colored laminates—makes this line of cabinets particularly pleasing. Manufactured by B&B Italia.*

Above *The* Apta *tables are ideal for a number of uses, such as coffee tables and sideboards. The wooden top is partnered by a rectangular tube frame in brushed steel or nickel-plated mild steel. Manufactured by Maxalto.*

philippe starck

M ad Genius–Showman is probably the best way to describe the prolific French designer Philippe Starck—he is a living phenomenon. Predictably unpredictable, he works in all fields of design including interiors, furniture, domestic artifacts, lighting and graphics—he has even designed motorcycles. Originally an architect, he is best known for the charismatic forms of his products.

Without constraint he seems to have single-handedly created an international design style that combines strong conceptual ideas, functional ingenuity, wit and provocative form with astonishing attention to detail. Not only does he look for innovative design solutions, he also combines this with an exploration of materials and process technology. The boldness of his irreverent approach, together with his sheer volume of work, has made him perhaps today's best-known and most noticed furniture designer.

The originality and lack of compromise in his work sometimes meant that it did not gain immediate public acceptance. However, his influence on all areas of the design industry and contemporary design itself is hard to refute. Perhaps he is better described as a sort of court jester, given his ability to imaginatively address real design issues in a charmingly light-hearted manner.

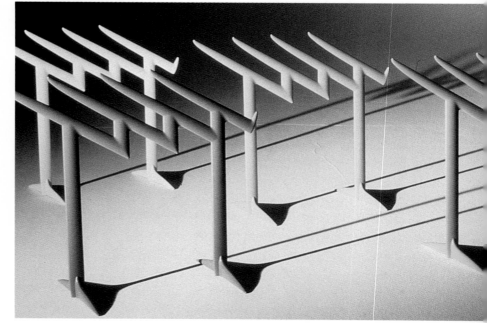

Opposite Claudia Evangelista *is an injection-molded plastic magazine rack. In this innovative solution, magazines are hung with their spines open over the plastic blades. Manufactured by Kartell.*

Right Romeo Moon *is a cast-fluted glass light fixture suspended from three steel wires. It is also available in fabric, in two sizes and in floor and table versions. Manufactured by Flos.*

Below Le Marie *is a clear and colorless polycarbonate molded seat shell with integral polycarbonate legs. Manufactured by Kartell.*

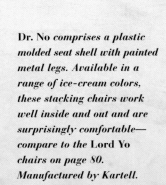

Dr. No *comprises a plastic molded seat shell with painted metal legs. Available in a range of ice-cream colors, these stacking chairs work well inside and out and are surprisingly comfortable— compare to the* Lord Yo *chairs on page 80. Manufactured by Kartell.*

jasper morrison

Known for the extreme clarity of his design solutions, Morrison has a serene ability to distill his works down with uncomplicated, elegant design solutions. Quiet and unassuming—quite the opposite of Philippe Starck—he studied furniture design at London's Royal College of Art. He quickly made his mark with early pieces, such as *Thinking Man's Chair* (see page 30), which established his cerebral approach to tackling design challenges.

In addition to his furniture designs, Morrison has worked at an international level on a wide variety of design projects including urban transport systems, architectural fixtures, household goods and tableware. All of his work bears the hallmark of severe sophisticated simplicity and an almost "Germanic Puritanism." His work typifies Mies van der Rohe's dictum, "less is more." He is most definitely the designer's designer.

Right *Lima Chair is constructed from plastic molded seat slats on a tubular metal frame. Manufactured by Cappellini.*

Right Bottle Rack, *designed for Magis, is made from injection-molded polypropylene with anodized aluminum connecting tubular substructure. A very simple idea using common components, this has been copied by many others but never improved upon.*

The nice thing about these Glo-Ball lights is that they are not completely spherical but are slightly squashed, like tangerines. This point was emphasized in their advertising campaign. Manufactured by Flos.

Above *The refined-looking organic aluminum forgings of the Lever Handle 1144 fit snugly into the palm. Actually designed for the contract market, this is nonetheless just as suitable for domestic applications. Manufactured by FSB.*

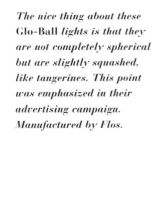

fact file tips on buying furniture

* Make sure that whatever you buy will fit through the front door and through all access routes to its resting point.

* Always test furniture for comfort, not just its looks.

* Make sure that a table can seat as many as you require.

* Check that the ticket price includes delivery and any sales taxes.

* Make sure that upholstery materials comply with fire regulations.

* Ask if customer's own material (COM) is an option.

* If the product is to be used outside, find out if it is made of suitable materials.

* Carefully check the item on delivery for faults and damage before accepting it.

* Remember that some furniture can take 8 to 12 weeks to arrive.

suppliers & designers

Stores and showrooms

The following stores stock a good range of contemporary furniture. If you are looking for a particular piece, telephone the store first to make sure they still carry the line.

AERO STUDIOS LIMITED
132 Spring Street
New York, NY 10012
Tel: (212) 966-1500 or
(212) 966-4700
Fax: (212) 966-4701
Retail store and interior design firm, not affiliated with Aero furniture manufacturer. Furniture by Eames, Gray, Nelson, Ponti and Florence Knoll; original designs by Thomas O'Brien; vintage pieces

ARKITEKTURA SHOWROOMS
560 Ninth Street
San Francisco, CA 94103
Tel: (800) 400-4869 or
(415) 565-7200, and
474 North Old Woodward
Birmingham, MI 48009
Tel: (800) 844-1126 or
(248) 646-0097
Classic modern furniture from Driade, Fiam, Flos, Fritz Hansen, Herman Miller, Kartell, Knoll, Vitra, Xo, Zanotta

JANE ATFIELD
244 Grays Inn Road
London WC1X 8JR, U.K.
Tel: +44 20 7833 0018

ATYS
306 South Main Street, 1D
Ann Arbor, MI 48104
Tel: (734) 996-2976
Fax: (734) 996-0220
E-mail: mail@atys-inc.com
www.atys-inc.com
Furniture by Aero, Alessi, Herman Miller, Mono, Starck

BLEU CITRON
www.bleucitron.com
Furniture by contemporary designers including Starck and Wadsworth Design, sold via web site

CASA DI OGGI
20385 Biscayne Boulevard
Miami, FL 33180
Tel: (305) 933-1022 or
(305) 933-2496
Fax: (305) 933-0955
European contemporary furniture from Moroso, Casprini, Arper, Malofancon

CONRAN COLLECTION
12 Conduit Street
London W1R 9TG, U.K.
Tel: +44 20 7399 0710
Contemporary furniture from Conran design team

CONRAN SHOP
Michelin House
81 Fulham Road
London SW3 6RD, U.K.
Tel: +44 20 7589 7401, and
55 Marylebone High Street
London BB7 1AA, U.K.
Tel: +44 20 7723 2233
Contemporary furniture from Conran design team and other designers

CURRENT
1201 Western Avenue
Seattle, WA 98101
Tel: (206) 622-2433
Furniture from Baleri, Bellini, Le Corbusier, Herman Miller, Aero, and others

DDC–DOMUS DESIGN COLLECTION
181 Madison Avenue
New York, NY 10016
Tel: (212) 685-0800
Fax: (212) 308-8795
E-mail:
ddc@interport.net
www.ddc-newyork.com
Furniture by Vico Magistretti and other European designers, and pieces by de Sede

DESIGN CENTRO ITALIA
1290 Powell Street
Emeryville, CA 94608
Tel: (510) 420-0383
Fax: (510) 428-1251
www.italydesign.com
Classics by Breuer, Mies van der Rohe and Le Corbusier; furniture by European designers

Secondhand shops are also a good source of contemporary furniture. George Nelson's seminal chair, whose organic form has been influential in recent times, was originally made by Knoll.

DESIGN WITHIN REACH
Tel: (800) 944-2233 for
catalog
www.dwr.com
*Furniture by Bellini, Breuer,
Eames, Nelson, Starck, Le
Corbusier, and up-and-
coming designers*

FORM@T
50 Wooster Street
New York, NY 10013
Tel: (212) 941-7995
Fax: (212) 941-5026
E-mail:
format4nyc@aol.com
*Closet design systems and
Italian furniture; pieces
from Moroso and Molteni*

**FREDERIC WILLIAMS
INTERIORS**
200 Lexington Avenue
New York, NY 10016
Tel: (212) 686-6390
*Furniture from Italian
manufacturers Molteni,
Minotti and Maxalto. To the
trade only.*

FULL UPRIGHT POSITION
Tel: (800) 431-5134 for
catalog
www.f-u-p.com
*Furniture by Bertoia,
Eames, Chadwick and
Stumpf, Saarinen and Le
Corbusier, and many others*

ICF GROUP
Tel: (800) 237-1625 for store
locations
www.icfgroup.com
*Furniture by Aalto (made by
Artek) and other European
designers*

IN-EX
1431-B Colorado Avenue
Santa Monica, CA 90404
Tel: (310) 393-4948
*Furniture from Molteni & C
and Ycami, and many others*

INFLATE
3rd Floor, 5 Old Street
London EC1V 9HL, U.K.
Tel: +44 20 7251 5453

INHOUSE
343 Vermont Street
San Francisco, CA 94103
Tel: (415) 554-1950
www.inhousesf.com
*Home office furniture,
lighting and accessories*

ITALMODE
32968 Woodward Street
Royal Oak, MI 48073
Tel: (248) 549-1221
*Furniture by Driade, Fiam,
Magis, Moroso, Vitra and
other European designers*

**JULES SELTZER
ASSOCIATES**
8833 Beverly Boulevard
Los Angeles, CA 90048
Tel: (310) 274-7243
Fax: (310) 274-5626
www.jules-seltzer.com
*Furniture by Eames, Flos,
Herman Miller, ICF, Knoll,
Thonet, Vitra and others*

LIMN CO
290 Townsend Street
San Francisco, CA 94107
Tel: (415) 543-5466, and
501 Arden Way
Sacramento, CA 95815
Tel: (916) 564-2900
www.limn.com
*Furniture by most top
contemporary designers*

LOFT
1823 Union Street
San Francisco, CA 94123
Tel: (415) 674-0470
Fax: (415) 674-0473
www.loft-sf.com
*Home and office furniture,
plus design services*

LUMINAIRE
301 West Superior Street
Chicago, IL 60610
Tel: (800) 494-4358, and
7300 SW 45th Street
Miami, FL 33155
Tel: (305) 264-6308
www.luminaire.com
*Furniture from Baleri Italia,
B&B Italia, Cassina, Driade,
Cappellini, DePadova, Flos,
Kartell, Magis, Maxalto,
Montis, Vitra, Xo, Zanotta*

THE MAGAZINE
1823 Eastshore Highway
Berkeley, CA 94710
Tel: (510) 549-2282
www.themagazine.org
*Furniture by Le Corbusier,
Miller, Jacobsen, Aero, and
many other designers*

MOBILI
2201 Wisconsin Avenue NW
Washington, DC 20007
Tel: (202) 337-2100
*Furniture and lighting from
Arco, Arper, de Sede, Flos,
Flou, Ligne Roset, Montis*

MODERN LIVING
8775 Beverly Boulevard
Los Angeles, CA 90048
Tel: (310) 657-8775
E-mail:
modliv@modernprops.com
www.modernliving.com
*Furniture by Aisslinger, Le
Corbusier, Starck, Cassina,
Flos, Moroso, Zanotta*

THE MORSON COLLECTION
100 East Walton Street
Chicago, IL 60611
Tel: (800) 204-2514 or
(312) 587-7400, and
31 St. James Avenue
Boston, MA 02116
Tel: (617) 482-2335
*Furniture from twenty-five
companies, including SCP,
and designs by Citterio*

NICEHOUSE
The Italian Centre Courtyard
Ingram Street
Glasgow G1 1DN, U.K.
Tel: +44 141 553 1377

OK STORE
8303 West 3rd Street
Los Angeles, CA 90048
Tel: (323) 653-3501
Fax: (323) 653-2201
*Furniture from Aero and
other products, including
Noguchi lamps*

O`VALE
2 Broad Street
Red Bank, NJ 07701
Tel: (732) 933-0437
Fax: (732) 933-0848
www.redbank.com/ovale
*Furniture and lighting by
Fritz Hansen, Knoll, Nelson,
Noguchi, Rietveld, Starck*

REPERTOIRE
114 Boylston Street
Boston, MA 02116
Tel: (617) 426-3865
Fax: (617) 426-1879
E-mail: info@repertoire.com
www.repertoire.com
*Furniture from Alias, Flou,
Cappellini, DePadova,
Driade, Flexform, Kartell,
Maxalto, Molteni, Moroso,
Xo; interior design services*

ROOM
151 West 30th Street
Suite 705
New York, NY 10001
Tel: (800) 420-7666 or
(212) 631-9900 for catalog
Fax: (212) 631-0153
www.roomonline.com
*Furniture by more than fifty
designers, including
S. Russell Groves and Aero*

SALON MODERNE
281 Lafayette Street
New York, NY 10012
Tel: (212) 219-3439
*Furniture by Italian
designers, including chaise
longue by Rodolfo Dordoni*

SEDIA, INC.
63 Wareham Street
Boston, MA 02118
Tel: (800) 228-4287
*Furniture by Le Corbusier,
Mies van der Rohe and
other modern designers*

SEE
920 Broadway
New York, NY 10010
Tel: (800) 258-8292 or
(212) 228-3600, and
8806 Beverly Boulevard
Los Angeles, CA 90048
Tel: (310) 385-1919
*Furniture from Edra, Flos,
Halifax, Horm, Kartell, Cor
line by Peter Maly, and
many other designers*

SONRISA FURNITURE
7609 Beverly Boulevard
Los Angeles, CA 90036
Tel: (323) 935-8438
www.sonrisafurniture.com
*Vintage and contemporary
steel shelves and storage*

TERENCE CONRAN SHOP
344 East 59th Street
New York, NY 10022
Tel: (212) 755-9079
Fax: (212) 888-3008
*Contemporary furniture
from the Conran design
team and other designers*

TRIOS HOME GALLERIE
1155 Canyon Boulevard
Boulder, CO 80302
Tel: (303) 442-8400
www.triosgallerie.com
*Furniture from Italian
manufacturers Arper,*

*Magis, Meccani, Molteni,
Moroso*

TROY
138 Greene Street
New York, NY 10012
Tel: (212) 941-4777
*Furniture by Aero and
Ou Baholyodhin*

VOLTAGE
2703 Observatory Avenue
Cincinnati, OH 45208
Tel: (513) 871-5483
www.voltageinc.com
*Contemporary and classic
modern furniture*

Manufacturers

AERO
96 Westbourne Grove
London W2 5RT, U.K.
Tel: +44 20 7221 1950, and
347-349 Kings Road
London SW3 5ES, U.K.
Tel: +44 20 7351 0511

B&B ITALIA U.S.A. INC
150 East 58th Street (main
U.S. showroom)
New York, NY 10155
Tel: (800) 872-1697 (for
nearest dealer) or
(212) 758-4046
www.bebitalia.it
E-mail: bbitalia@nyct.net

BLANK AND CABLES
615 Indiana Street
San Francisco, CA 94107
Tel: (415) 648-3842
www.blankandcables.com
*Original furniture by Walter
Craven and others*

BOND PROJECTS U.K. LTD
Prism Design Studio
38 Grosvenor Gardens
London SW1W OEB, U.K.
Tel: +44 20 7730 3011

BRUETON
979 Third Avenue
(showroom)
New York, NY 10022
Tel: (800) 221-6783 or
(212) 838-1630 for local
dealers
Fax: (718) 712-6783
E-mail: start@brueton.com
www.brueton.com
*Contemporary furniture by
Stanley Jay Friedman and
other designers*

CAPPELLINI MODERN AGE
102 Wooster Street
New York, NY 10012
Tel: (212) 966-0669
www.cappellini.it
*Showroom for Cappellini.
Furniture by Aisslinger,
Dixon, Irvine, Lissoni,
Morrison, Pillet, Ruhs and
other designers*

CASSINA USA INC.
155 East 56th Street
(showroom)
New York, NY 10022
Tel: (800) 770-3568 (for
nearest dealer) or
(516) 423-4560
www.cassinausa.com

CO-MOTION
960 Howard Street
San Francisco, CA 94103
Tel: (415) 512-1043 or
433-6336 for catalog
Fax: (415) 433-6330
*Furniture by Andy Hope
and others*

**DE SEDE OF
SWITZERLAND**
2001 West Main Street
Suite 157
Stamford, CT 06902
Tel: (800) 688-7112 (for
nearest dealer)
Fax: (203) 353-1799
*Contemporary and classic
leather furniture*

DIALOGICA
484 Broome Street
New York, NY 10013
Tel: (212) 966-1934 (for
nearest dealer)
Fax: (212) 966-2870, and
Von Demme
1690 Union Street
San Francisco, CA 94123
Tel: (415) 441-1696
*Contemporary furniture,
rugs, lighting and linens by
in-house designers*

FLEXFORM
Tel: (800) 763-6767
E-mail: flex@flexform.it
www.flexform.it
*Furniture by Citterio, Paolo
Nava and in-house designers*

FLOS USA
200 McKay Road
Huntington Station, NY 11746
Tel: (800) 939-3567 (for
nearest dealer) or
(516) 549-2745
Fax: (516) 549-4220
*Lighting by Morrison and
other designers*

FLOU
Tel: (514) 932-8880
Fax: (514) 932-6616
E-mail: info@flou.cq.ca
www.flou.it
*Furniture by Vico Magistretti,
Studio Sigla, Vittorio Prato,
sold at Limn and DDC stores*

FORMA & DESIGN
Tel: (203) 855-9325 for local
Fiam dealers
Fax: (203) 855-1360
Furniture by Starck and Fiam

S. RUSSELL GROVES
270 Lafayette Street
Suite 502
New York, NY 10012
Tel: (212) 966-6210 or
(212) 966-6269
Original modern pieces

HERMAN MILLER, INC.
855 East Main Avenue
P.O. Box 302
Zeeland, MI 49464
Tel: (888) 874-0045 or
(800) 646-4400 for store
locations and dealers
www.hermanmiller.com
*Home and office furniture
by Chadwick, Eames,
Nelson, Noguchi, Stumpf,
and other designers*

HILLE INTERNATIONAL
Cross Street
Darwen
Lancashire BB3 2PW, U.K.
Tel: +44 125 477 8850, and
Business Design Centre
52 Upper Street
London N1 OQH, U.K.
Tel: +44 207 288 6202

HITCH-MYLIUS LTD
Alma House, 301 Alma
Road
Enfield
Middlesex EN3 7BB, U.K.
Tel: +44 20 8443 2616 or
+44 20 8443 2617

HOLLY HUNT, LTD
275 Market Street
Minneapolis, MN 55405
Tel: (800) 433-4038 or
(612) 332-1900
Tel: (800) 446-1313 for local
dealers
Fax: (612) 332-6179
*Furniture by Christian
Liaigre and other
contemporary designers*

KARTELL
45 Greene Street
New York, NY 10012
Tel: (212) 966-6665
www.kartell.com
*Furniture by Ron Arad,
Citterio, Magistretti and
Starck*

KNOLL
Tel: (800) 445-5045 for local
dealers
www.knoll.com
*Furniture by Bertoia,
Breuer, Gehry, Saarinen,
Mies van der Rohe and
other classic designers*

LIGNE ROSET
Tel: (800) 297-6738 for store
locations or catalog
www.ligne-roset-usa.com
*Furniture by Pascal
Mourgue, Didier Gomez and
other European designers*

LUCE INTERNATIONAL
300 Beale Street, Loft 415
San Francisco, CA 94105
Tel: (800) 591-3222
Fax: (415) 543-3211
E-mail: luce@sirius.com
www.lucecontract.com
*Lighting from European
contemporary designers*

MONTIS
Tel: (888) 866-6847 (for
nearest dealer) or
(336) 861-7768

PALAZZETTI
515 Madison Avenue
New York, NY 10022
Tel: (888) 881-1199 or (212)
832-1199 for showrooms
Fax: (212) 832-1385, and
3211 Oaklawn Avenue
Dallas, TX 75219
Tel: (214) 522-1111
Fax: (214) 522-9867
E-mail: info@palazzetti.com
www.palazzetti.com
*Wide range of
contemporary furniture*

PUCCI INTERNATIONAL
44 West 18th Street
New York, NY 10011
Tel: (212) 633-0452
Fax: (212) 633-1058
One-of-a-kind and limited

*edition furniture, such as
geometric shelf units by
Chris Lehrecke, and the
Écart furniture collection.
Open mainly to the trade.*

ROCHE BOBOIS
Tel: (800) 972-8375 for
store locations or catalog
www.roche-bobois.com
*Contemporary furniture by
in-house designers*

SMART FURNITURE
Tel: (888) 762-7841
www.smartfurniture.com
*Simple, customizable stor-
age systems and furniture*

**UNIFIED STUDIOS FOR
DESIGN AND
ARCHITECTURE (USDA)**
3450 Sacramento Street
San Francisco, CA 94118
Tel: (800) 681-USDA
*Furniture by Christopher
Deam, Daven Joy, John
Randolph*

VITRA
557 Pacific Avenue (West
Coast showroom)
San Francisco, CA 94133
Tel: (800) 338-4872 for
local dealers, or
(415) 440-3720
www.vitra.com
*Furniture by Citterio,
Gehry, Nelson and others*

VITSOE
85 Arlington Avenue
London W1X 9FB, U.K.
Tel: +44 207 354 8444

**Vintage and secondhand
furniture**

EMMERSON TROOP
7957 Melrose Avenue
West Hollywood, CA 90046
Tel: (323) 653-9763
Fax: (323) 653-5445

E-mail:
emmtroop@aol.com

GALILEO
37 Seventh Avenue
New York, NY 10011
Tel: (212) 243-1629

MIAMI TWICE
6562 SW 40th Street
Miami, FL 33155
Tel: (305) 666-0127

MODERNICA
7366 Beverly Boulevard
Los Angeles, CA 90036
Tel: (323) 933-0383
E-mail:
modernicala@earthlink.net
http://members.aol.com/
modernica1

OUTSIDE
442 North La Brea Avenue
Los Angeles, CA 90036
Tel: (323) 934-1254

WELL-DESIGNED
6550 SW 40th Street
Miami, FL 33155
Tel: (305) 661-1386

Auction houses

**BUTTERFIELD &
BUTTERFIELD**
220 San Bruno Avenue
San Francisco, CA 94103
Tel: (415) 861-7500

CHRISTIE'S
502 Park Avenue
New York, NY 10022
Tel: (800) 247-4558

EBAY ONLINE AUCTIONS
www.ebay.com

SOTHEBY'S, INC.
1334 York Avenue
New York, NY 10021
Tel: (212) 606-7000

Places to visit

COOPER-HEWITT NATIONAL DESIGN MUSEUM
91st Street and Fifth Avenue
New York, NY
Tel: (212) 849-8400

MUSEUM OF MODERN ART
11 West 53rd Street
New York, NY 10019
Tel: (212) 708-9400

SAN FRANCISCO MUSEUM OF MODERN ART
151 Third Street
San Francisco, CA 94103
Tel: (415) 357-4000

ART INSTITUTE OF CHICAGO
111 South Michigan Avenue
Chicago, IL 60603
Tel: (312) 443-3600

FRANK LLOYD WRIGHT HOME AND STUDIO
951 Chicago Avenue
Oak Park, IL 60302
Tel: (708) 848-1976

ROBIE HOUSE (designed by Frank Lloyd Wright)
5757 South Woodlawn Street
Chicago, IL 60637
Tel: (773) 834-1847

FALLINGWATER (designed by Frank Lloyd Wright)
Mill Run, PA 15464
Tel: (724) 329-8501

DELANO HOTEL (interiors designed by Starck)
1685 Collins Avenue
Miami Beach, FL 33139
Tel: (305) 672-2000 or (800) 555-5001

WASHINGTON DC–DULLES INTERNATIONAL AIRPORT (designed by Eero Saarinen)
Tel: (703) 572-2700

FARNSWORTH HOUSE (designed by Mies van der Rohe)
14520 River Road
Plano, IL 60545
Tel: (630) 552-8622
www.farnsworthhouse.com

Further reading

Thomas Hauffe: *Design.* Barron's Educational Series, 1996.

The Work of Charles and Ray Eames: A Legacy of Invention. Vitra Design Museum, Harry N. Abrams, 1997.

Francois Baudot: *Eileen Gray.* Thames & Hudson, 1998.

Tom Dixon. Architecture, Design and Technology Press, 1990.

Jasper Morrison: Designs, Projects and Drawings 1981-1989. Architecture, Design and Technology Press, 1990.

Starck. Benedikt Taschen Verlag GmbH, 2000.

100 Masterpieces from the Vitra Design Museum Collection. 1996.

Penny Sparke: *Furniture: Twentieth Century Design.* E.P. Dutton, 1986.

Leslie Pina: *Fifties Furniture.* Schiffer, 1996.

Leslie Pina: *Furniture 2000: Modern Classics and New Designs in Production.* Schiffer, 1998.

Ugo La Pietra: *Gio Ponti.* Rizzoli, 1988.

Alan Crawford: *Charles Rennie Mackintosh.* Thames & Hudson, 1995.

Charlotte & Peter Fiell: *Modern Chairs.* Benedikt Taschen Verlag GmbH, 1993.

Charlotte & Peter Fiell: *1000 Chairs.* Benedikt Taschen Verlag GmbH, 1997.

Arthur C. Danto & Jennifer Levy: *397 Chairs.* Harry N. Abrams, 1988.

Mel Byars: *50 Chairs: Innovations in Design and Materials.* Rotovision, 1997.

Mel Byars: *50 Tables: Innovations in Design and Materials.* Watson-Guptill, 1997.

Peta Levi: *New British Design 1998.* Mitchell Beazley, 1998.

Edward Lucie-Smith: *Furniture: A Concise History.* Thames & Hudson, 1988.

Pocket Design Directory. Janvier Publishing, 1998.

Phillippe Garner: *Sixties Design.* Taschen America, 1996.

Alexander von Vegesack: *Thonet: Classic Furntiure in Bent Wood and Tubular Steel.* Rizzoli, 1997.

Lynn Gordon: *ABC of Design.* Chronicle Books, 1996.

George H. Marcus: *Design in the Fifties: When Everyone Went Modern.* Prestel, 1998.

Vico Magistretti's **Flower Chair** *is similar in shape to* **Incisa** *(page 11). This petite piece is made in a manufacturing-friendly manner without losing its sophistication. Manufactured by DePadova.*

index

First published 1999 by Conran Octopus Limited, a part of Octopus Publishing Group, London. North American edition published 2000 by Soma Books, by arrangement with Conran Octopus.

Soma Books is an imprint of Bay Books & Tapes, 555 De Haro St., No. 220, San Francisco, CA 94107.

For the Conran Octopus edition:
Commissioning Editor: Denny Hemming
Series Editor: Gillian Haslam
Managing Editor: Kate Bell
Creative Director: Leslie Harrington
Art Editor: Lucy Gowans
Stylist: Emma Thomas
Production: Zoe Fawcett

For the Soma edition:
North American Editor: Karen O'Donnell Stein
Proofreader: Ken DellaPenta

Library of Congress Cataloging-in-Publication Data
Conran, Sebastian.
    Soma Basics—furniture / Sebastian Conran & Mark Bond; photography by Thomas Stewart.—North American ed.
        p.cm.
    Rev. ed. of: Conran octopus contemporary furniture. 1999.
    Includes bibliographical references and index.
    ISBN 1-57959-015-2 (pb : alk. paper)
        1. Furniture—History—20th century. I. Title: Furniture. II. Bond, Mark. III. Stewart, Thomas. IV. Conran, Sebastian. Conran octopus contemporary furniture. V. Title.
NK2395 .C65 2000
749.2'049—dc21
                                                    99-054438

Printed in China
10 9 8 7 6 5 4 3 2 1

Distributed by Publishers Group West

Acknowledgments

Special thanks to Tim Gadd for research and for all his help behind the scenes. Thanks, also, to Kathryn Mills and Helen Thompson.

The authors and publishers wish to thank the following for their considerable help and assistance: Alexis Nishihata at **Aero**; Linda Gledstone at **Atrium**; Edward Barber and Jason Osgerby at **Barber Osgerby Associates**; Andrew Stafford at **Bedfordshire**; Marcus Stevens at **Bisley**; Gill Hicks at **Blueprint**; Clemente Cavigioli at **Cavigioli**; Annabel Buckingham and Nick Cooney at **Coexistence**; Jamie Abbot at **Conran Holdings**; Abigail Bond, James Peto and Eric Kentley at **Design Museum**; Elena Graves at **Eurolounge**; Nicholas Howard; Peter Lewis at **Function**; Jonathon Sherwood at **Haus**; Colin Shergold at **Herman Miller**; Lindsey Nicolson at **Hille International**; Jane Atfield at **Kiosk**; Sarah Cottan at **Knoll International**; Vallery McInnes at **McInnes Cook**; Andrew Harrold and Sara Jones at **Nicehouse**; Luke Pearson and Tom Lloyd at **Pearson Lloyd**; Joanne Leyland at **Purves & Purves**; Piers Roberts and Fiona Dodd at **Same**; Sheridan Coakley at **SCP**; Simon Alderson at **Twenty Twenty One**; James Mair and Tamara Caspersz at **Viaduct**; Natalie Keuroghlian at **Vitra**; Mark Adams at **Vitsoe**; Anna Burnett at **Wireworks**.

We would also like to thank the following people for allowing us to photograph their homes and premises: Ou Baholyodhin, Sharon Bowles of Bowles & Linares, Joe Hagan, Mei Teck Wong and Juan Dols of Dols Wong Architects.

With thanks to the following for the kind loan of transparencies: **Andrew Stafford** (p.76–77 photo Tariq Dajani), **B&B Italia** (p.80 bottom and p.115 *Apta* table), **Atrium** (p.34 *21 Hotel Grand Suite* chair), **Cappellini** (p.59 *Juli*), **Cassina** (p.9 *Wink* chair photo Andrea Zani), **Coexistence** (p.90–91 *Jason* sofa and p.115 *Domusnova*), **The Conran Collection** (p.46 *Arion* bar stool and p.70–71 *Loop* table), **DePadova** (p.11 *Incisa* chair and p.125 *Flower* chair photo Luciano Soave), **Driade** (p.88–89 *Refolo* cart photo Emilio Tremolado), **Flos** (p.115 *Lastra* light), **Lucy Pope** (p.50 *Powwow* table), **Jasper Morrison** (p.118–119), **Ron Arad** (p.55 *Fantastic Plastic Elastic* chair), **Studio Citterio** (p.114 portrait of Antonio Citterio by Gitty Darugar), **Twenty Twenty One** (p.121 *George Nelson* chair), **Viaduct** (p.39 *King Tubby*, p.46 *Cheap Chic* bar stool, p.52 *Cam El Eon* chair, p.65 *Olivier* chair), Vitra (p.24 *Wiggle* chair, p.28 Eames chair, p.31 *How High the Moon*, p.36 Eames *Lounge Chair and Ottoman*, p.54 *Ply* chair, LCW chair and *Panton* chair, p.59 *Meda* chair, p.64 *Coconut* chair, p.112–113 coat rack and portrait of Charles and Ray Eames), **Vitsoe** (p.75 *606 Universal Shelving System*).

Thanks to the following companies for the loan of additional furniture and acessores for photography: **LSA International** (1932 789721), **Purves & Purves** (20 7580 8223), **Aero** (20 7351 0511), **Same** (20 7247 9992), **Alma Home** (20 7377 0762), **Egg** (20 7235 9315), **Space** (20 7229 6533), **Maxfield Parrish** (20 7252 5225), **Habitat** (645 334433), **Eurolounge** (20 7792 5477).